PRAISE . ...
IT'S YOUR CAREER, IT'S YOUR CHOICE

"Before even turning to the first page, the title of Mark's book reinforces lessons of necessity to find the right position with the right company. In my own 40-plus career years in workforce development, I can reiterate that the focus should always be on YOUR choices. Each chapter describes a developing roadmap of personal development toward targeting end goals. Mark's experience and application certainly benefit career seekers. The sections that discuss Veteran transition to the civilian workplace are critical insights. Read — absorb — take notes — apply."

—Michael Dolphin, retired Chief of
Workforce Services, State of California

"Mark Brenner has once again displayed his acumen when it comes to career preparation and development. His years of experience in various industries will assist the reader to fine-tune their knowledge, skills, and abilities for success in the competitive marketplace for talent. I have had the pleasure of working with Mark as he helped transition veterans that have returned to school. He as translated what he does in person to an incredibly useful text. Kudos for an excellent read!"

—Dr. Salvador Esparza Professor and Chair, Department
of Health Sciences, California State University

"Mark has been a competitor collaborator for over 30 years. Anybody interested in advancing, changing or starting a career would benefit greatly from Mark's knowledge, experience, innovation and strategic approach to building a career. I am honored to recommend and confident his guide will be a valuable tool."

—Kent Stastny, retired Sr. VP The Yoh Company, Exec
VP Bartech and Sr VP Acro Service Corp.

"This is the best book on career choice that so completely outlines what you need to do to get in with the right company and the right position. This is a must read for anyone who is looking for their first career opportunity or who wants to transition from their current career."

—Steven H. Stumpf, EdD, CSUN Health Administration

"Through this book, Mark and Mary have developed a practical and no-nonsense approach to helping you land your ideal job. They help each reader define a career path that works. This book will help you identify your passions and interests, career values, ideal industries, and the work environments where you can excel. Their step-by-step guide empowers you to define your specific path and the steps to get there. Whether you are a seasoned veteran or just starting out – this book will help you achieve your goals."

—JD Darby Vice President of Operations, ConnectBase

"As someone who has coached many stressed job seekers, I wish I had this book to give to my clients. Mark and Mary lay out a step-by-step process that takes out all the stress and leaves in all the joy of finding the right job. A must read if you are right out of college looking for your first job or transitioning after 40 years. Bravo Mark and Mary!"

—Shaya Kass, PhD, Life Coach

"Look no more for THE Step-By-Step approach to obtaining your dream job. The authors have complied all you need to present yourself properly to employers through writing an appealing resume to interviewing and asking the right questions to achieve your career goals. Mark and Mary provide many tips on standing out from the competition to get selected. This is the Guide you've been looking for and scanning the Table of Contents will make you buy this book. You won't be disappointed!"

—Michael Weinper PT, DPT, MPH President PTPN, Inc.

IT'S YOUR CAREER IT'S YOUR CHOICE

A Step-by-Step Approach to Choosing the
RIGHT CAREER, then Landing the
RIGHT POSITION with the RIGHT COMPANY

MARK BRENNER WITH MARY GOMEZ

It's Your Career, It's Your Choice: A Step-by-Step Approach to Choosing the Right Career, Then Landing the Right Position with the Right Company
Published by 5 Star Publishing Group, LLC
Los Angeles, California

ISBN: 978-0-578-31686-4
BUSINESS & ECONOMICS / Careers/Job Hunting

Publisher's Cataloging-in-Publication Data
Names: Brenner, Mark, author. | Gomez, Mary, author.
Title: It's your career – it's your choice : a step-by-step approach to choosing the right career, then landing the right position with the right company / Mark Brenner with Mary Gomez.
Description: Includes bibliographical references. | Los Angeles, CA: 5 Star Publishing Group, 2022.
Identifiers: ISBN: LCCN: 978-0-578-31686-4
Subjects: LCSH Career development. | Job hunting.| Career changes. | BISAC BUSINESS & ECONOMICS / Careers / Job Hunting
Classification: LCC HF5382.7 .B74 2022 | DDC 650.14--dc23

Cover and Interior design by Victoria Wolf, Wolf Design and Marketing. Copyright owned by Mark Brenner & Mary Gomez

To the most important people I know:
Adrienne, Emma, Maggie, and Miles
Doreen, Karen, Sam, Claire, and Chole
And Jason

And to Mary's Mom, Dad, and son Anthony

CONTENTS

ACKNOWLEDGMENTS

Mark's Acknowledgments

Perhaps the most important acknowledgment in preparing this book goes to my partner, Mary Gomez — her contribution by writing parts of every chapter, her compliments and constructive feedback, and her dedication to making this book what we believe will be a universal roadmap to find the right career with the right company. With over seventy-five years of staffing and human resources experience between us, we have tapped into decades of work to help people identify their career of choice and learn the best and most efficient way to navigate the hiring process.

I would be remiss not to recognize Robert Schwartz, Joe Winklebauer, and Sid Richter who gave me my start in the staffing industry. And there were other inspiring people who pushed and encouraged me to make this step: Lynn Parker whose words changed my life and the way I view the world, Kent Stastny who stood by me regardless of my faults, Katie Phelan who even though she had no idea helped me achieve many of my successes, and to my dear friend Eileen Gold who after sixty years still wants to be my friend.

There are so many others to thank and acknowledge, because they have all had a profound effect in molding my life — so many but to name a few

— thank you to Ravel Montgomery, Terry Giangreco (RIP), Jeri Kashkin, John Muzzalupo (RIP), Melissa Liefer, Melody Garcia, and Mary Norton.

Mary's Acknowledgments

Mark Brenner, you are my "Quan." Thank you for being patient, kind and, over the years, my greatest mentor and most importantly, my friend. You were the first person who gave me a chance in the staffing industry, and with your guidance and expertise I excelled as a professional and achieved more in my career than I thought I ever could.

To my son, Anthony — do what you love and love what you do. Remember, whatever you choose to do in life live well, be healthy, take chances, and for God's sake STOP to smell the roses. Life is short — live it well and give-'em hell!

CHAPTER 1
Why Is It Important to Choose a Career?
Here's Mark's Story...

I HAD A GOOD CAREER. I made good money. Yet now as I look back on forty years in the same industry, I ask myself, "What was I thinking?"

So let's go back to 1965. I was seventeen and in my last year of high school. I had already decided I wasn't smart enough to go to a four-year university and was taking only those classes that would get me through the next six months. So I did not sign up for the SAT test and did not apply to any college, even though my parents thought I had done so. It would be easy to blame my parents or my teachers. (I was always told I had potential but was not using it — I guess I did not want to use up my potential.) But, as I look back, I find I was just too lazy — I did not like school, I did not like to study, and I just got by! I wanted to be social and talk about how I was going to become a lawyer. I was a debate club star and could always argue my way out of any situation. But something inside told me that it would never happen — I was just too damn lazy!

After high school I moved with my family from Los Angeles to New York City. I had no plans; I just did not care! Sometime in August of that year, as I was strolling through the East Village in Manhattan, it dawned on me that

1

perhaps I should go to college. I quickly returned to Queens and applied to the local community college. It was August, and classes started in September. I was accepted to night school with four classes.

Around this time I met a very pretty and smart girl. I was so enamored with her that I spent all my time with her and, of course, neglected my schooling! The result: I failed all four classes! What to do now?

I got a job as a jewelry salesman at some store in Jamaica, Queens. If there is any job in the world that is worse than boring, it is working at a store where there are only two or three customers each week. I spent my nights going to bars (you know, being social) and drinking too much, with no direction and no ambition.

It's the late 1960s, and this was the time of the military draft! I had no exemptions from the draft and did not even think to get one. My closest friend just joined the U.S. Army, and I thought this option might be best for me. And like every other decision I have made in my life, I consulted no one! So I talked to the Army (I did not want to go to Vietnam), the U.S. Marine Corps (they promised I "might" get out of basic training alive), the U.S. Navy (I just didn't like the uniforms), and the U.S. Air Force. So I joined the Air Force.

The next three years and eight months were absolute hell! I was a clerk, subjected to anti-Semitism and racism. Then I "pissed off some officer" and was sent to Vietnam — well that's another discussion for another time. The one thing I learned in the Air Force was that I would not be a career military person. For the first time I wanted to make something of my future. (Ironically almost forty years after I was discharged, I created a nonprofit organization that coached Veterans as they transitioned from active duty to a civilian career.)

It's now December 1969. I got married and moved back to California (the marriage did not last long). For the first time in my life, I was determined to be somebody — I needed to get my undergraduate degree and go to law school. First, I was off to community college and then to a university. In less than three years I received a bachelor's degree in political science. I was going to apply to law school.

But there was one problem: I was broke! No savings and no one to ask for money. I was living with my grandmother in a one-bedroom apartment, and I had a car that was one gallon away from falling apart. My father was pressuring me to GET A JOB! I was twenty-five years old, and he felt that I was already too old to find a career! Maybe it was guilt or maybe my laziness was creeping back into my mind, but I went looking for a job.

So I got a job. My advisor at college referred me to a person who ran the Southern California division of a "job shop." What the hell is a job shop? Today it's called a staffing company. I was hired as a recruiter of technical people who would work on a temporary basis for a company. Whoever heard of such a thing? And for someone who has a hard time putting together anything that says "some assembly required" I was now recruiting technical people — aircraft engineers, designers, mechanical and electrical designers — with all sorts of skill sets I never knew existed.

But it was 1973, and I was making money: $100 a week! And honestly, I enjoyed being a recruiter. I love talking with people, and this was a perfect place for me. So I put off law school for another six months or so ... big mistake! The company I worked for was a small company based out of New Jersey and run by one of the brightest, no-nonsense persons I have ever met. He helped mentor me and was a great inspiration. I stayed as a recruiter, and after less than one year I was making a whopping $300 per week. Who needs law school?

Over the next four decades, I remained in the staffing industry. There were a few detours where I tried to do something else. I went to broadcasting school and was licensed to become an announcer or a disc jockey, but after sending out twenty audition tapes I gave up. I worked for almost one year as a stockbroker, but when a staffing company called and offered me $35,000 a year I quit and moved to the San Francisco Bay Area.

And I was on my way! By 1980, I was promoted and was the youngest vice president in this national organization and was running the Southwest region. The money was good, and the job was fun. Who wouldn't have fun taking clients to dinner, traveling, and being part of a big corporation with all the perks? Law school was a distant thought — besides, I was thirty-three years old, and who wants to spend three years back in school? Big mistake!

In 1985, I was recruited by a former colleague to run his newly founded staffing company — damn, I would be president of the company. So I moved to Chicago and began my upward corporate movement. I had left my daughter and wife in Denver, and I was commuting between the two cities every two weeks. But after a few months I realized that either I was too lazy to become a success or that the owners were less than honest. It turned out to be both. After six months I returned to Denver, and for the first time in twelve years, I was looking for a job.

At this crossroads in my life I had a great reputation, and it was not long before I had three job offers. Two were in California and one was in New York. I accepted a position in California as a branch manager. Wow, I'm thirty-six years old, have been a vice president of a very large company and president of a small company, and now I'm a branch manager! The money was OK, and I knew the person who would be my boss. I was back in Southern California, so I was content. It was easy, I knew the business, and I was likable, so I was promoted to vice president after three years. And again, I got to travel and work in an industry that I knew.

I worked directly for one of the original founders of the company. I can say without reservation that he was not the best of bosses — every day was worse than the next. He made working a chore, and I was extremely unhappy.

After six years I had had enough. I started putting out the word that I was looking to move to a better company. I was recruited by a testing company that wanted to start a staffing division. I accepted the job with a hefty salary increase and, along with my best friend, we were going to make our mark in the staffing world. The story gets complicated and is too long to explain (trusting your best friend is sometimes devastating), but suffice to say I was only with the testing company for eighteen months before I was ready to move to my next job.

A position with another staffing company allowed me to be introduced to the CEO and president of the largest staffing company in the world. I reached out to the president and began discussions with him about creating a new division for the company. After a few months, they made an offer, and I accepted. I found myself moving to Northern California. This was the best job I have ever had! I was surrounded by intelligent and outgoing senior executives, and I knew I was on my way to a dream career … until the company merged with another large staffing firm, and my position was eliminated.

So now I'm forty-seven with no job and a reputation that had been beaten down by inference and truth. I was recruited for a position as the senior vice president of a mid-size staffing company in the San Francisco Bay Area. My tenure with this company ended after a little over two years when I decided to open my own staffing company.

And I did. Along with my now ex-wife, we found money to start our own staffing company. We launched our business in June 1999, and for twelve years we ran our own business. The business was successful, and I was able to grow the company to a point where I could offer it for sale. The sale was completed in 2012, and I agreed to work for the new owners for three years. Another big mistake!

Almost immediately I realized that they had bought my business and not my expertise. Fast forward five months, and we parted ways. To make a long story short, there were attorneys and false claims and, in the end, I walked away with about one-third of what I had expected. I was upset about the money but not about leaving the staffing industry. After forty years I was burned out and, as I reflected on my career, I wished I would have gone in another direction. For the most part, I didn't put effort into directing and shaping my career. I simply moved from one job to the next. And I continually disregarded my dream of going to law school.

I was sixty-three and just sold my business. I didn't have enough savings to retire and, even if I did, I don't think I could play golf seven days a week.

What next? Do I get a job? Do I start a business? For the first time in my life I started thinking about what I should do that would make me happy.

After hundreds of hours of research, I made the decision to become a Coach — a Career Coach, an Executive Coach, and a Business Coach. After all, I essentially spent forty years doing just that. This was the "social" part of my jobs that I truly enjoyed. It was time to put my experience to work to help others who may be having an issue with their career, help leaders in their ability to manage people, and work with business owners to improve businesses that need help.

As I continued to conduct my research, my newly hatched career plan somehow evolved into working with Veterans. I'm not sure how I got there, but it dawned on me that Veterans who were transitioning from the military had little if any idea how to get a job once they separated from service. This was my new calling! I had an idea for a Veteran's coaching program and researched nationwide to see if anyone was doing the same or even similar work. To my surprise, I could find no one organization that would create customized individual career coaching programs for Veterans. Of course, there were large organizations that would work with Veterans to find positions once they separated from the service, but not one organization that would customize a program specifically for the needs of each Veteran.

So I started a nonprofit that would work with Veterans and assist them as they started looking for a civilian job, called Veterans Career Xchange. I attended every Veteran event in Southern California, networked with other Veteran nonprofits, and I was on my way. In the first year, I coached over 200 Veterans with a 90 percent success rate of coaching Veterans to help them identify and land jobs in their chosen careers. I spent most of my time coaching and spent the remaining time trying to raise funds to finance the nonprofit. During the first two years I raised enough money to hire a staff. This was a good fit for my skill set and was an extremely rewarding career. I knew that if the donations and grants kept coming into the organization, I would be doing this for a very long time.

When I began the nonprofit for Veterans in early 2014 the unemployment rate for Veterans was more than 15 percent. Surprise! By late 2015 the Veterans unemployment rate dropped to just over 6 percent. Suffice to say there is a correlation between donations and need. The need dropped significantly and, by the end of 2015, my donations tapered off and grants for smaller Veteran nonprofits were few and far between. But I loved what I was doing — I wanted to continue as a Coach!

I had started Brenner Career Management in mid-2015 as a placement company to complement my nonprofit. While I did not want to get started again in the staffing industry, it was a great way to add income and work closely with my nonprofit to place Veterans in good jobs. As the unemployment rate for Veterans decreased that year — and the decrease in donations followed — I decided to turn Brenner Career Management into a Career, Executive, and Business Coaching organization. I truly enjoyed coaching, and this was the perfect transition from working with Veterans in my nonprofit to working in the private sector.

I networked and found a few coaching referral websites and was able to establish a solid client base. As it turns out, I have been coaching my entire working life. Now I could use forty years of experience to help my clients find the right career, navigate the hiring cycle, become a better and more effective manager, or build a business that is profitable and successful.

So this is how I got here. It has been quite a journey. Yes, there are regrets, but overall it's been a great ride! Lessons learned. For me, a major lesson is knowing that everyone should understand how to choose your career — the right career — whether it is your first job, a better job, or a completely different job. Keep reading! We will discuss everything necessary, so the decisions you make are comfortable and lead you on a path to success.

This is not a how-to book! It presents a step-by-step approach to choose the right career and take the necessary steps to find the right position with the right company. Many self-help books are written by someone who has succeeded and who wants to share their experience, so you too can benefit from their success. This book is different. Although I succeeded in a career, it was one that chose me — not one I planned for! As I reflect on my forty years in the staffing industry I look back and say, "What was I thinking? I should have put more thought and effort into my career. I should have been more deliberate about my choices. And I should have directed and shaped my career to pursue my goal of becoming a lawyer to ensure a sense of fulfillment — without looking back on a career that is tinged with some regrets."

As an expert in staffing and hiring, I learned the steps necessary to have a successful career. In this book, you'll find a proven approach to make sure you select the right career or transition to the right position in the right company. In the chapters that follow, you will find the most efficient way to navigate the hiring cycle and find the fulfilling position or career you want.

Over the past twenty years, the process of hiring has undergone a complete metamorphosis, and this book will ensure you understand the steps necessary to find your place in the career you want. After you have completed each chapter, you will know how to choose your career and how to get the job you want. You must always remember this entire process is about YOU!

Further, we will discuss how the COVID-19 pandemic has affected the job market and the manner in which hiring is conducted. In the aftermath of the pandemic we are seeing a shift from a large percentage of onsite work to a hybrid work model that, in some cases, equally combines onsite and remote work. Plus, the interviewing process is changing rapidly from in-person interviews to video interviews. These video interviews take on a new dynamic of interviewing.

Many organizations and human resource companies that are dedicated to supporting human resources have written papers and articles about resumes, networking, and interviewing. This is the one, single source for the entire process from choosing a career to navigating the hiring process to getting hired. We have created this comprehensive career book with over seventy-five years of combined human resource, staffing, and coaching experience. No one can do it better.

Let's get started!

CHAPTER 2

Your Career, Your Choice

MAKING A CAREER CHOICE can and should be one of the most important decisions in your life. There are a few other decisions you will make that will be just as important: getting married, buying a house, having children, and deciding when to retire. I'm getting ahead of myself when we start discussing retiring — first we need to decide on a career.

This choice is both objective and subjective. On the one hand, researching and discussing your possible career goal is only part of your decision. The decision to move forward with your choice is quite subjective, and you must be careful not to let your emotions get in the way of your decision. My father once suggested that when making any decision, I should write down all the positives and negatives about my impending choice. It did not take much time to realize that if you really want something and try to be objective, you will always find ways to make a choice the way you want it to be. So creating a balance between subjectivity and objectivity is difficult, but it can be done with the proper mindset.

Long ago, you may have decided to become a professional such as a doctor, lawyer, accountant, engineer, computer programmer, or golfer. (Yes, I wanted to become a professional golfer, and today I am rated 3,484,690 in the world — wrong career and possibly no talent!) If you have not decided on a career choice, let's set the stage. Which of these three common scenarios is similar to your situation?

1. You have just graduated from high school, and you are not sure if you want to go to college. You get a job at a low wage, but the benefits or perks are good. After promotions and wage increases over a few decades you are ready to retire! Is this what you wanted? Is this the career you would have chosen for yourself? Perhaps not. What if you understood how to select a career that would give you all you wanted, and you could look back and say, "I had a great career"?

2. You have recently graduated from college, and you just don't know what you want to do. You attend Career Day at your college, and all the big companies, government agencies, and a few smaller companies are there looking for management trainees. You decide in the heat of the moment (or after a day or two of soul searching) that you want one of the positions that were available during the career fair. You apply for a job in an area you had never previously considered. You go through the interview process, and you get hired. At first you enjoy what you are doing, because it is new and exciting. You receive a couple of promotions, and you are well thought of in the company. You stay. But over time the job becomes redundant, and it is an effort to go to work each day. But you remain at the company, because your position is secure and financially rewarding. And forty years later you look back and say, "What was I thinking?" This is what happened to me — don't let it happen to you!

3. You have been in a position after high school or college for a few years, and you feel that this is not the right career for you. You have decided to make a change and want to use the experience you have

gained to transition your career. But to what? How do you decide? You don't want to make a wrong choice, so you research other industries and companies to find what you think is the right career path for you. This choice encompasses two factors that need to be considered: Is this a long-term decision, and am I passionate about the decision?

The career choice you make can be a life-defining decision. Finding the right position with the right company is hard work. Take time to understand what you want to do, and pursue it! Just accepting the first or second offer for a position without the passion and soul searching can possibly result in regret as you look back on your career. You're looking for your career niche, but accepting the first position offered may not be the right choice. It is easy to take a new position and start making money. And it's a great feeling to know that a company wants you to work for them and is investing in your future. But your career choice is not about a company — it is about YOU. Now is the perfect time to look at who you are and what you want to become.

Someone once said to me that no one ever planned to become a toll booth operator as they were discussing the next steps in their career (no offense intended to all the toll booth operators). Was there a time in your life when you had an idea of what you wanted to be "when you grew up"? Perhaps there was an outside influence, or someone suggested you might choose another career. Life rarely follows a straight line — there is always something that occurs that will change your direction. Perhaps it is a family emergency, the need to get a job now and make some money, or hundreds of other events that alter our career paths. But most of us make important decisions and then an event occurs unexpectedly, and we are now on another course and a career we never even dreamed of having.

Remember the movie *The Graduate* and the word *plastics*? A business executive offered this unsolicited career advice to the main character, Benjamin (a recent college graduate): "There is a great future in plastics." There was no sequel, so we will never know if Benjamin decided to work in the plastics industry, but you could tell by his reaction that he wasn't very interested in pursuing plastics!

My outside influence was my father. And his comments are part of the reason I made the career choice I did and now, so many years later, I still regret it! I was twenty-five years old and yes, I was broke, but I wanted to go to law school. My father made a not-so-subtle comment that I was twenty-five and had no job and no career — and it was time for me to GET A JOB!

I am not sure if I was reacting out of guilt or the fact that I was twenty-five and broke, so I decided to find a job. (Let's agree that the world has changed in the past forty years and being twenty-five years old is not too old to find out what you really want to do with your career.) Fast forward forty years, and I was still in the same industry. Interestingly, almost thirty years later my daughter asked if I thought she should go to graduate school and get a master's degree. Remembering my father's comment and how it affected my life, I simply said, "It's your decision." Even though I did not think it was the right time for her to leave the state for graduate school, I did not want to be the influence that caused her to not pursue her dreams.

Outside influencers can make an innocent comment that can change the course of your life. A long while ago a friend of mine, who was passionate about becoming a photographer (he had already been accepted to the Brooks Institute of Photography in Santa Barbara, California) took some of his work to a famous photographer. He asked this photographer to review his work and was told that there was a difference between a "photographer" and a "picture taker." He told my friend he was a good picture taker! Suffice to say my friend was devastated and decided to pursue another career. In many cases someone's subjective review of your life's passions can cause you not to pursue your dreams. My friend always regretted not pursuing his dream, and I could sense a bitterness in him. As it turned out, he became a corporate executive and just retired a few years ago. Yet after a successful career in business, he told me he will always regret not becoming a photographer!

Between outside influencers and life's events sometimes we end up on a different career path. We need to explore and make a plan — life is not a rehearsal. You have a career decision to make, so take time to make the right choice. Experience has shown that it is quite difficult to change careers after investing so much time in your first career choice. Change is difficult and career change can feel impossible. This first part of *It's Your Career — It's Your Choice* is dedicated to helping you find a career that is a fulfilling career you can look back on and say, "I made the right choice."

Deciding On a Career

You want a career that is satisfying and financially rewarding. What are your passions? What are your interests? Identifying your passions and interests is the key to finding a career that you can be proud of and one that you want. I am not a psychologist, but I do know that finding the right career can be an important key to your happiness. A great family life with all the activities you experience can only be better with the choice of a fulfilling career. I personally know folks who get stuck in a career and are unhappy. In my case, my career choice did not align with my passion (other than the coaching aspect) and, unfortunately, it had a negative effect on my family life.

How do you make this choice? As mentioned above, there are two factors you must consider as you decide to move forward with your career: your passions and interests. I can't tell you how many times I have heard my coworkers say, "I hate this job." You probably know some folks who have been in a job for decades who, without hesitation, will tell you they despise going to work. They do so, because they feel stuck, they have financial obligations, and they think they cannot afford to make a change. These people end up settling and just passing time until they can retire.

Remember, you need to make an intelligent and informed choice about your career. If the choice is wrong, make sure you take immediate action to correct it. Waiting a day, a month, or even years to make a change can result in accepting a career you did not really want. Don't get stuck. Take this important step now to find the right career.

When deciding on your career path, you will need to match your passions to the job market. The job market is always cyclical, but there are always careers in certain sectors. The first step is identifying an industry in which you may want to work. Over the many years of working with job seekers, I have found many professional information technology and engineering folks who will not work in the defense industry. Whether it is a social choice or for any other reason, they have made the choice to work outside this industry. Choosing an industry is simply done through research. You can conduct in-depth research on the Internet, access a wide variety of resources at your local library, and talk with friends, family members, and neighbors about their careers.

Look at a variety of different industries and find one or two that are of interest to you. Once you decide on these industries it is now time to look at a few of the companies who are the leaders in their field. Remember that for every company in every industry there are vendors that support the company's work. For example, if you have decided to work in the automotive industry, General Motors has thousands of outside vendors that supply this major manufacturer with parts and every conceivable piece of equipment imaginable. Business author Tom Peters once wrote, "Outsource everything" — and almost thirty years later most companies are outsourcing a great amount of the work they once had supplied in-house. For every industry and for every company in that industry there are thousands of opportunities.

In the following chapters we will show you how to overcome your lack of experience in a specific industry and begin your career in the area in which you want to work. Perhaps the most important theme of this book is for you to realize that your career is about YOU! When a company has an opening for a position for which you may be qualified, they are going to hire someone whom they believe is qualified. It may or may not be you. So this is not about the company — it is about YOU! Ask yourself: Is this position right for me?

Is this company right for me? Is the company's culture a good fit? Do I really want the position? It is YOUR decision.

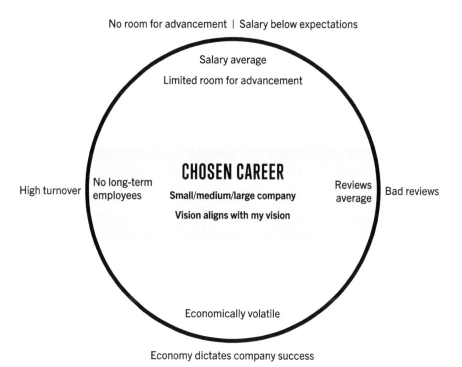

CIRCLE OF ACCEPTANCE
MY CAREER

No room for advancement | Salary below expectations

Salary average

Limited room for advancement

High turnover

No long-term employees

CHOSEN CAREER

Small/medium/large company

Vision aligns with my vision

Reviews average

Bad reviews

Economically volatile

Economy dictates company success

Perhaps the best way to process the decision on your career is to use my Circle of Acceptance. (You may have heard of the circle of influence, and this is basically the same concept but it relates to your career.) The Circle of Acceptance places your ideal career choice in the center of the circle. This is the job and career you want with an ideal salary and benefit package. It is a long-term decision. As you leave the center of the circle, perhaps the position you are considering does not offer the salary you were expecting or the benefits. Or this may not be the right position in the right industry but, overall, it is acceptable. Once you leave the inner circle you will leave your area of acceptance. This means you can immediately eliminate this company and position as they are not the right fit for you.

Take a few minutes — right now — to draw YOUR Circle of Acceptance. Think about the industry you want to work in, the position you want to hold, and your salary and benefit requirements. At this stage in your career search, you may not be able to fully complete your Circle of Acceptance with all the details, but this is a start. And this book is all about getting you started on your career path, so you can land the right position with the right company.

The choice of an industry and a company requires research to ensure they are aligned with your passions and interests. Of course, there are times you are going to make a career decision based on your current situation, economics, and your life in general. Yet to choose what you want to do in an industry you want to work in could be considered a perfect career decision. However, regardless of the amount of research you conduct and the decision you make, it could over time turn out to be the wrong one! If you find this is the case, don't hesitate to make a change. Remember, the longer you wait the more difficult it will become to make a career change.

So many people I have encountered in my life remain in their positions because of economic and family issues. Most of these folks are unhappy and just getting by, because they are convinced they have to stay in their jobs. We spend on average eight to ten hours a day, five days each week working. Considering the average commute is forty-five minutes each way to work, we are spending almost ten hours or more a day in work mode. If we sleep eight hours each day, we only have about six hours (or less) each day to enjoy our lives outside of work. Given the time-consuming responsibilities of raising children, grocery shopping, cooking meals, and doing household chores, that does not leave a lot of time! There is no work/life balance!

The most important reasons to research and decide on a career that is right for you are ensuring that your workdays are fulling and that your time outside of work is enjoyable and productive, without continually feeling exhausted or frustrated by your work. If we look at work productivity, the more you are in the right career the more productive you will be. I remember I had a man working for me years ago who was up for his first review. During his review I let him know that his performance was substandard and, if it did not improve, I might have to terminate his employment. I was shocked by his response, "Well if you paid me more, I would be more productive." Suffice to say he was not in that position very long. Yet this does suggest that a great number of people who are working are in their jobs solely for financial reasons and not because this is what they want to do.

In another instance, I terminated a trainee recruiter, because he was not productive. He was bright and worked hard but had no desire to be in the staffing industry. This attitude directly impacted his productivity. Some twenty-five years later, when we reconnected, he was a senior human resource executive at a major Silicon Valley firm — that was the first time someone ever thanked me for letting them go.

As I look back on my career, I know I could have made a change to a variety of positions in numerous industries, but I was comfortable and afraid to leave the staffing industry. Being comfortable and afraid is no excuse for staying when you know you can do so much more. Don't let comfort get in the way of your happiness. After forty years in the same industry, I truly regret not making a change sooner. When I sold my staffing business I conducted a great deal of research and decided to become a Career Coach. Looking back, it was the best career move I ever made.

Become passionate about what you like and what you want to do. Research by reading, talking to people you know, and get introduced to people who work in those industries you are passionate about. (Chapter 5 is dedicated to networking, which is by far the most important part of finding the right position.) If you are unsure about your career direction, some companies offer a job-shadowing option, so you can better prepare yourself for your career choice.

Don't allow yourself to fall down the proverbial rabbit hole by staying with the same job and the same company if you are not happy. Maintaining a work/life balance is an important decision to consider. A position where you are overworked (even though you are compensated well) will have a damaging effect on your life. In addition, many of us need to be recognized and rewarded for our efforts. This recognition can come in many forms: financial, promotion, awards, or perhaps the proverbial pat on the back. But if you are not happy or you are overworked, what toll does it take? If that toll is affecting your health, your family, or your job then it is definitely time to make a career transition.

If you enjoy your job but not the company, make the decision to find a similar position with a different company. But make sure you research the company and the people, so you do not find yourself in the same situation again. If you don't like the company and don't like what you are doing in your job, perhaps it is time to transition your career. Simply switching to the same or similar job in another company might not be the solution. As they say, the grass is not always greener on the other side of the fence!

Career Transition

You may be five, ten, fifteen, or twenty years into your career, and you feel that you do not want to spend the rest of your life in the same job or or at the same company. Or you may feel as if you are in a rut. You may want to make a change, but you may be afraid and you may have family responsibilities and financial obligations. You might find it almost impossible to take that first step to a rewarding career. By remaining in a position that you know is not right for you, everything else in your life will be affected. I know of very few people who can completely separate their careers and family life. Identifying a career that is right for you is a choice and, although extremely difficult, it can help create that work/life balance we all crave. By ignoring your work/life balance you are letting your negative career experience define you.

During my time as a Career Coach, I have worked with clients who are at various stages of their careers who want to make a change. Some felt they were working in a position with no future or financial upside. In a few instances my clients enjoyed the work they were doing but wanted to use their experience to work in a different industry. In every instance they made a decision to improve their career by finding a position that would make them happy. As you contemplate a career transition, understanding how to best make this happen is the key to your success.

The following case studies can help you understand the different approaches to transition your career. If you are transitioning to a completely different career, the key to making this transition is networking with individuals who work in the area in which you have interest. If, however, you are transitioning from one company to another in the same or a similar field, the approach will be a combination of networking and researching to find the right company. Let's look at a few case studies.

One of the first clients I coached was a senior information technology project manager in government consulting. He was in his mid-fifties, so making a career move was not easy, especially when he wanted to transfer his vast experience to the healthcare industry. He also wanted to move from being a project manager to a program manager. His situation was further compounded by the fact that he lived on the West Coast and was commuting to the East Coast every week. The demanding weekly travel was having a negative effect on his health and his family life. He had two requirements: change industries and find a position that was local.

We first developed a resume that included all his relevant experience and coupled it with his passion for working in the healthcare field. We also updated his LinkedIn profile to reflect his experience and his passions. (As you will see in Chapter 3's discussion on resumes, you can never be untruthful, but you can accentuate certain points to highlight your passions!) The secret to successfully make this transition was identifying a few healthcare organizations in the region and subsequently networking within the industry.

Over the course of three months he actively networked and connected with C-level executives, directors, and managers at local healthcare organizations. One connection led to another, and he eventually spoke with a vice president at a nationally known consulting company. This connection introduced him to another vice president in the company who ran the healthcare division. During the next six weeks he participated in four interviews. Suffice to say, he was offered — and accepted — a position as a program manager in the company's healthcare division and is no longer traveling each week.

In another instance a client was working as a high school teacher for over twenty years and no longer wanted to be associated with education. We spent weeks determining the best course of action to find the career that would make his life everything he dreamed of. After talking out his fears and passions we concluded that there is a huge similarity between teaching high school students and many activities conducted in companies' human resource departments. But making this transition was going to be difficult, as he had no human resource experience, and he needed similar compensation to support his family.

This is where transitioning a career into an area where you have little, if any, experience can be difficult. Searching for open positions in human resources and submitting a resume that does not show relevant experience is the first step to rejection. It was important that we prepare a resume that reflected his teaching experience and also discussed some of the similarities between the two positions. But more importantly (as we will discuss in the chapter on networking) he needed to network with organizations that were on his list of targeted companies. It is important to understand that without the specific job experience, he had to connect with someone at his targeted companies to explain his desire to work in human resources and explain how his similar experience could be an asset to the organization. By using our networking techniques he was successful and, within a few weeks, he had scheduled a series of interviews that resulted in a new position and a new career.

Another coaching client held a master's degree in clinical psychology. She did not want to take the time and effort needed to pursue a PhD, which is often a requirement for a career in clinical psychology. She decided to apply to nursing school and become a nurse. After two years working as a nurse, she decided this was not a match after all and reached out to me. After giving her career much thought, she wanted to be a researcher. Although she had minimal experience in this area we set out on a course to find the right research position in her part of the country. We developed a resume that discussed her experience including some of the research work she completed while going to school.

As in most cases when making a career transition, she needed to find a networking stream that would get her introduced to a company and the decision makers, so she could explain her qualification to become a researcher. After an extensive networking campaign, she found a company on the West Coast that was looking for a remote researcher in her area. She had experience in that particular area of research, and it seemed like a "slam dunk" for her to interview for the position and, ideally, receive an offer.

She identified the hiring manager from a LinkedIn search and contacted him. After a phone meeting, they both agreed she was perfect for the position, but she needed to send her resume to human resources for review. Three days after submitting her resume to human resources she received a stock rejection letter letting her know she was not qualified for the position. She was devastated! Not one to give up quickly, I helped her by reaching out to the human resources manager through LinkedIn and scheduled a discussion with her. I questioned the manager to learn why she rejected the resume. After reviewing my client's background and experience she informed me that "Oops, I must have missed this one." In the end, everything worked out, as my client interviewed and received a job offer and, at the time of this writing, is still a full-time employee with this organization.

Unfortunately, this sequence of events is classic in today's job market, since we are dealing with applicant tracking systems (ATS) and human resource screeners who do no more than quickly scan the resume they are expected to read and carefully consider. With all due respect to everyone in the recruiting profession, it is understandable that after reviewing hundreds of resumes there will be a time when you may not see that a particular candidate may be qualified. Perhaps with the advancement in applicant tracking systems these kinds of errors will be eliminated.

In another example, my client was unhappy with the career path he had chosen. In fact, he was so discontent as a CPA, he applied to and was accepted in a graduate program at a local university in its school of public policy. He had spent over twenty years as a CPA. Although I would like to believe that age discrimination does not exist — it does!

Yet there are ways that networking can eliminate any consideration for age as a negative factor. He wanted to work for the government or a government contractor to improve the communication between policy and the public. He was committed to working in a position that would allow him to do "the greater good." He spent a great deal of time researching companies and government organizations that would have a need for his background and expertise. He reached out to dozens of managers at consulting companies. Prior to contacting government agencies he researched www. USAjobs.com (the federal government's official employment site) to see what opportunities existed. After identifying over fifteen positions that he would be interested in, he sought out decision makers who worked for these agencies.

Sending a resume to consulting companies and government agencies was an exercise in rejection. His experience and work history would not show his passions and his true career goals. Again networking was the key to his success. Scheduling a conversation would allow him to express his desire to work in public policy. Suffice to say, after a few weeks of networking and holding multiple lengthy conversations he was able to secure an interview and was offered a position as a public policy advisor. He has been in this position for over three years and is thriving, doing the job he wanted.

I have dedicated Chapters 4 and 6 to applicant tracking systems (ATS), online job boards, and recruiters. There are unique and effective ways to navigate an ATS, make the most of the hundreds of online job boards, and find specific ways to work with a recruiter for your benefit. Each one of these steps will help you make the transition of your career easier and more effective.

When you know you are qualified and the right person for the position, don't give up after a rejection. There is an art in getting a potential employer to know who you are and what you can do for them. There is a fine line between being assertive and being aggressive. Be assertive and persistent, but don't become an annoyance. We will discuss in depth how to be assertive in the chapters on networking and interviewing.

As we continue this journey, our discussions will center on your ability to attract the attention of an employer even though you may not have the specific experience needed for the position. The hiring process is cyclical. In a great job market there are an abundance of open positions and enough qualified candidates to fill the positions. In a down job market there are few jobs with an abundance of candidates. And finally, when the unemployment rate is lower than five percent there is usually an abundance of jobs with very few qualified candidates.

When the unemployment rate is low the job market offers the best opportunity for career transition. Companies will create a job description that includes all the necessary skills to perform in the position, but their requirements are flexible since there may be few perfectly qualified candidates when the unemployment rate is low. For example, if there are ten requirements necessary for the position an organization may relax its requirements and only require six of the necessary skills. So as you are exploring transition options you may find yourself qualified for the job you want.

Transitioning your career can be a life-changing event. Finding your niche and enjoying each day is a wonderful feeling. For over forty years in the staffing industry, I don't think I ever truly enjoyed working in the business. Sure, I loved working with people, finding opportunities to coach people, taking clients to dinner, playing golf with customers, and being the boss. But much of the work was tedious and redundant. I was caught up in the fact that I was an executive and making fairly good money, and I was afraid to even consider a transition.

When I finally sold my staffing business and was no longer working in the industry, I found a niche in career coaching. This is what I should have done twenty years earlier! For me, the transition happened in the twilight of my career. Coaching was everything I knew I was good at — I was able to take my years of experience and help others find the right career and a fulfilling position. Yes, I regret not making this change sooner, but let's not live in the past. It's easy to say to yourself, "I should have done this" or "I should have become a lawyer, doctor, or something I would have truly enjoyed." But you didn't — I didn't. Let's move on. It's time to become what you want to be.

If you are serving (or have served) in any branch of the military, be sure to read the following section — we included it specifically for you! If you are not a Veteran, skip to the next section, which addresses a critical aspect of the career search: time management.

The Veteran's Transition

This part of the chapter is dedicated to everyone who has served in any branch of the military. Thank you for your service!

As a Vietnam Veteran and the founder of a nonprofit organization that assists and coaches Veterans as they transition from the military to a civilian career, I know it can be a difficult leap from military life to a career in the private sector, but your transition doesn't have to be difficult when you have the right tools and realistic expectations in place.

When I was discharged from the U.S. Air Force I knew I wanted to finish college and become a lawyer. I immediately applied to colleges in California (I was discharged on the East Coast) and was accepted to a university in Southern California. For the next three years I worked part time and attended college full time. I graduated with honors three years later. As I mentioned earlier in this book, my dream of becoming an attorney was dashed, because I was broke and needed a job! Accepting what I thought then was a temporary job as a recruiter became a forty-year career.

If you are leaving (or have left) the military, deciding on a career or transitioning a career is not an easy task. Yet I know you probably are excited about the possibilities of a civilian career. After I spent three years in a military environment, the thought of finding a civilian position and career was quite intimidating. On the one hand, you may have had a military position that is far from what you see yourself doing once you separate from the service. Or perhaps you want to pursue the same kind of work you were assigned while you were a member of the military. Either way, pursuing a civilian career can be a great adventure that will shape the rest of your life.

The U.S. government has worked hard to develop programs to prepare you for life after the military (for example, the Transition Assistance Program and other related programs). These programs are designed to make your transition to the "real world" seamless. The programs are designed to inform you of your benefits, the differences between military and civilian life, and how to adjust to civilian life once your separation date arrives. Part of the program discusses your civilian career and preparing to find the right position with the right company.

These programs are well designed; however, they spend a limited amount of time discussing your future career choice and goals. They may briefly outline the hiring process, so you can be prepared for a civilian position. Usually there are resume templates and a list of employers that focus on hiring Veterans. But navigating the hiring process in today's digital world is difficult for separating Veterans. These programs serve the purpose for which they were designed — to make your transition to civilian life as seamless as possible. This book will give you all the tools necessary to find the right career with the right company.

I have coached over 400 Veterans, many of whom did not have any idea of what they wanted to do once they separated from the service. Of course, you may have a clear career path such as working in security, law enforcement, or another position that is closely related to your military job. A high percentage of those who separate from the military believe they have few options about career direction.

One of the Veterans I coached had spent over twenty-five years in the U.S. Army as an infantryman and felt he had no transferable skills to the private sector. In fact, his resume mentioned his combat missions and the types of weapons he used in his daily tasks! (We will discuss later in this section about what should and should not be included on your resume.) Further, when we talked he would always confirm our meeting time in "military time." For example, if we were going to speak at 4:00 p.m. he would confirm that we were speaking at 1600 hours.

Perhaps the biggest challenge when transitioning from the military to a civilian career is being able to adapt to the civilian workforce. In the military, the rigidity of the daily workday does not transfer to the private sector. So one of the first changes that needs to occur is accepting that you are no longer working under a chain of command that demands your adherence to a strict code of conduct.

This is not to say that you won't need to show respect for your supervisors in the private sector, but the differences between a military position and a position as a civilian are vastly different. In the military, you are required to perform under circumstances that are rigid and exact without, in most cases, the ability to state an opinion or be creative.

After a series of coaching sessions with the infantryman I realized that this was not the only job he had in the service. As we discussed his work, we discovered he had also spent time handling supply services. When asked about his future, he was excited to learn that there may be a place for him in a company as a supply chain analyst. We then put together a resume that discussed his work in supply chain. He started networking, and he was almost immediately accepted for an interview. After we conducted extensive interview training, he met for his interview and was accepted for a position with an aerospace company where he is still employed today. This is an example of how unsure many separating service members are about their careers and unaware of their transferable skills as well as what path they should take.

In the private sector, companies may welcome your feedback and suggestions. Some companies even ask their employees to be innovative and "entrepreneurial." In the military, your feedback and suggestions may be met with resistance. I distinctly remember making a suggestion in the Air Force, only to be told, "This is the way we have always done this task, and that is what we will continue to do." Making this mindset adjustment can be difficult, especially if you have spent over ten years in the military. If you have spent only a limited time in the service, the adjustment can be much easier.

After spending time in the service and working with hundreds of Veterans who are making the transition to a civilian career, I have found that there are not many non-government outlets to help transitioning Veterans find the right career. Of course there are dozens of organizations that hire "case workers" to assist Veterans as they seek career opportunities in the private sector. Some of these case workers have little experience or understanding about how to identify the right career or guide you through the hiring process.

You don't need a case worker! You need a career specialist — a Career Coach! You need to adapt to the differences between military and civilian life, and you need someone to guide you through the hiring process. As you look for a career specialist make sure you are comfortable with the person. Don't hesitate to interview two or three career specialists and choose the one who you feel will benefit you the most. The right career specialist is your partner and your guide to assisting you in finding the right position.

My nonprofit was dedicated to one-on-one coaching that identified career opportunities for transitioning Veterans and then showed them the process necessary to find the right position. Keep in mind that the larger Veterans organizations that are nonprofits are funded by grants and donations. Their main interest is making sure that they meet their "grant or donation quotas." That is to say they are more interested in putting you to work to satisfy requirements of their donors than having you find the career that is right for you. Don't get me wrong, there are hundreds of dedicated case workers who look out for their clients' best interests as they transition to a civilian career. It is just that, in many instances, they have little, if any, experience in guiding and helping their clients find the right career. By using the tools in this book, you can be assured that you will know how to identify the right career, the right company, and the right position.

Once you have made the "cultural" transition from the military to civilian life, you can begin your search to find the right career. Using the Circle of Acceptance to help you identify your career choice is your first step to finding the career you want. Gaining an understanding of your goals and your passions will enable you to select a career path that will have you on your way to a successful and rewarding position in the industry you have selected.

It is easy and comfortable to accept a job with a company that pays you a decent wage. Remember, selecting a career can be exciting. Settling for a job just because it pays well may have you looking back years from now thinking you could have done better. Take the time necessary to discover your passions and know what you want to do. Many companies will go out of their way to hire Veterans, so it is incumbent on you to seek out the companies and positions you want.

Let's take a minute to discuss companies and their hiring initiatives. Many mid-size and large companies have Veteran hiring initiatives. Some organizations like to say they have a Veterans hiring initiative when in fact they do not — in today's environment it is a politically correct statement. Other companies with government contracts have a quota that they are required to meet regarding the number of Veterans they need to hire. Usually it is a percentage of their total workforce. In either case, however, private companies will hire the most qualified candidate for an open position. Never take for granted that because you are a Veteran you will be hired by a company who has a Veteran hiring initiative. I have not seen a case where a Veteran was hired who was not also qualified for the position.

As the founder of a nonprofit focused on Veterans, I spent time speaking with companies and colleges about how they can work with the Veteran community to make sure that, collectively, we make every effort to decrease the Veteran unemployment rate. It was interesting that a large percentage of folks at the colleges and companies I spoke with were hesitant to speak about or hire Veterans. In fact, some of these folks outright told me they were fearful of hiring Veterans due to their combat experience.

In one very strange case, I spoke with the person responsible for hiring Veterans at a major university in Southern California. He told me he would not hire anyone who had been in combat or had carried a weapon! I guess my shock was evident. I ended our conversation abruptly and never referred anyone to him again.

Earlier I spoke of the infantryman who had listed the types of weapons he used while he was in the Army. My experience with hiring managers and companies that hire Veterans is that you should never talk about combat, weapons, and missions. Of course you should let them know about your time in the service but leave the specifics out of your resume and conversations, so you do not take the chance of upsetting or scaring an interviewer. Use the resume template presented later in this book to create a resume that will be attractive to potential employers.

During most of my Veteran coaching sessions I was asked, "How soon prior to my separation should I begin looking for a job?" As a rule of thumb, private-sector companies will not usually hold a position open if your separation date is more than three months away. But now is a great time to begin identifying the type of work you want to do and the companies for whom you want to work. Once you have selected an industry and identified companies in that industry, you can begin your research to find the specific companies with whom you want to work. (Factors can include region, whether they have a Veteran hiring initiative, cultural fit, and so forth.) Chapter 5 will show you how to use LinkedIn to identify employees of the specific companies you identified and begin connecting with them.

Using the networking model presented in Chapter 5 will almost immediately have you speaking to someone at the preferred companies. Once you explain your situation (for example, you are currently in the military and are planning on separating from the service in a few months), you may find that the companies that are "Veteran friendly" will ask you to contact them once you have been discharged. By making these connections, management at many companies will be impressed that you reached out to them. You have made a connection and may possibly have a job opportunity once your separation date arrives.

If your separation date is a month away this is a good time to begin contacting the management of the companies you have chosen. Have your resume ready for submittal to a potential employer and be prepared to be asked for an interview. Be sure to keep reading. The guide to networking success and preparing for your interview are detailed in Chapters 5 and 7.

One final note, it is against federal law for anyone to ask you about your discharge status. For example, if you have an honorable discharge or a discharge that is less than honorable, you cannot be asked about the reasons. The only exception is if you were dishonorably discharged for a felony.

Follow the steps in this chapter to make a career choice. Once you have chosen a career path you can use the following chapters to understand how to find the right position with the right company.

Time Management

What is the definition of time management? Primarily, this is analyzing how you spend your time and prioritizing tasks to maximize your personal efficiency in the workplace and at home. Let's break this down when it comes to the job seeker's definition of time management.

Time management takes practice and consistency. The key here is to set challenging but achievable goals and eliminate any obstacles that could possibly get in the way. Good examples of obstacles or distractions are smartphones, social media sites, or unnecessary family interruptions. Establish a consistent routine and set time limits and boundaries for social media and family activities. It is important to eliminate distractions, as they can be a huge productivity killer. If you are a social media junkie and you look at your phone 100 times a day, then put away your phone during the times you have set aside for your job-search activities.

Your job search must be a priority, and the amount of time dedicated to your search should be added to your daily, weekly, and monthly plan of action. When thinking about effective time management, think about setting goals that are challenging, attainable, and measurable. When looking at your goals, prioritize specific tasks based on importance. Take a look at Stephen Covey's Time Management Matrix (a popularized version of Dwight D. Eisenhower's Urgent-Important Matrix). Use this, and I can assure you that your time will be well spent. Planning is so important. If you set aside two to four hours each day to complete specific job-seeking tasks, before you know it, you will begin to see a higher level of activity and results. Filling your pipeline with connections and companies will help yield the right career opportunity.

Let's touch on multitasking for a minute and why NOT TO DO IT! I am great at multitasking. That said, I found that when multitasking I started projects that were never finished, or I didn't have time to devote my full attention to the project, so it ended up not being my best work. My advice: focus on one task at a time. Finish that task and move on to the next item on your daily plan.

Just for a minute, let's come back to prioritizing tasks, organization, and documentation. Several free customer relationship management (CRM) tools can help a job seeker stay on track, focused, and organized. For example, I have found HubSpot to be very user friendly. By developing a time management plan of action, you can streamline your job-search journey. Personal CRMs can help you organize tasks by priority, compile a list of target companies, and compile a list of key contacts. In addition, you can set up to-do lists to track your daily, weekly, and monthly tasks and schedule appointments and reminders. This tool is an effective way to streamline your search efforts and keep yourself on subject and organized. You can find other notable CRMs by conducting a simple Google search and reading reviews to see which option would be best for you.

Depending on how long you have been looking for a job, you may be feeling like the job search is a full-time job but without the paycheck! Personally, when I think about time management, I think about how effective I was at my job and how structured my schedule was. At the time, it was important for me and the team that I managed to have a plan of action set every day. I remember preaching that "without a plan of action you have no purpose or direction." If you have no plan you are just reacting. Your time-management plan needs to create a balance between being both proactive (for example, searching to discover open positions) and reactive (for example, immediately submitting a resume when you uncover a great opportunity).

When you have a plan of action in play and you know what your purpose is, you begin to feel as though you've actually completed and accomplished something that you set out to do at the end of each and every day. Perhaps you have been recently impacted by a layoff or some other circumstances beyond your control. If so, having purpose can help with the sudden impact of having too much idle time on your hands.

To this day, the feeling I have when I can put a checkmark next to my high-level priorities gives me a sense of continued accomplishment. At the end of each day, planning for the next day and moving tasks around based on their priority level continues to be a fun routine. Your daily action plan can and will change depending on the day, circumstance, and those things that are out of your control. But having a plan and the ability to be nimble is essential to continually move forward.

Our schedule tends to be a moving target. I feel a sense of accomplishment when looking back through the days, weeks, and months and seeing what I have tackled and eventually can mark off my to-do list and, of course, looking at what still needs to be done pending priority. For me, this is about having some sense of control over my time. Most likely, your day will never turn out exactly the way you thought it would. My point is you need to be flexible and expect the unexpected in your daily work life. And looking for a job is no different. Having an action plan will help to keep you focused on the important things such as where you want to devote your time and job-search effort.

You are probably asking yourself this question: "How much time should I spend on my job search?" Your question is valid and depends on you and your circumstance. For example, if you were recently laid off and received a severance package, you may have the luxury and time to find the right opportunity. But what if you were laid off without receiving a severance and now rely heavily on your savings or unemployment? Now, time is not on your side and finding a job needs to be your focused priority. Whatever situation you are faced with, having a well-thought-out plan is key to your success and finding the position you want.

Devoting a structured amount of time researching companies, reading through job posts, tweaking your resume to fit the job posting, filling out profiles, networking, and submitting your resume can be exhausting. By creating a daily time management plan, you can eliminate the stress associated with your job search.

To have a successful job-seeking experience it is important to set yourself up right in the very beginning of your job search by creating a daily, weekly, and monthly action plan. Without a plan you can easily lose focus and — before you know it — your severance package, unemployment benefits, or both will run out. DON'T PROCRASTINATE! As a job seeker, you would like to be doing anything but sitting in front of a computer scouring through hundreds of job postings looking for a job. So let's break down this scheduling thing even more.

For example, ask yourself if you are an early riser. Do you like to get up before the sun rises and have everything on your list done by noon? If this sounds like you and the beginning of the day is when you are most productive, incorporate your job search into your daily morning routine. It's important to focus on important and challenging tasks when your productivity is highest. You can save simpler, less important tasks for times in the day that you're less alert. Decide in advance how many hours in the day you are going to devote to your job search. If you are a late sleeper and tend to be a night owl, then structure your job search during those times, but whatever you do have a plan and stick to it.

Evaluate each day and prioritize accordingly. Schedules will change and so do priorities — work on the most important tasks and leave the less important tasks for later in the day or week.

By planning at the beginning of your job search you will save yourself time and frustration during the process.

Here are a few suggestions to consider at the outset of your job-seeking journey to create the best plan for you:

- Decide how many hours in a day is a reasonable amount of time based on your "life schedule" to devote to your job search. From there, you can begin to develop your daily, weekly, and monthly plan.

- At the beginning of each week, you could focus on interacting with online job boards and employer websites, filling out profiles/applications, and connecting at a higher level with a company's leadership team.

- Tuesday is a great day to engage with an agency recruiter or targeting past alumni. If you are interested in working at a start-up company, you could explore and target private equity and venture capital organizations.

- Wednesdays could be used to expand your company target list and research new industries and emerging markets or perhaps connect with past teammates and supervisors. As your plan develops over time you will begin noticing where you are gaining the most traction. Adjust your plan accordingly to fit your weekly results.

- Where do you want to focus your search: LinkedIn, job boards, professional network, employer websites? And what type of jobs are you gravitating toward?

- Are you looking to change industries and, if so, what other profession or industry are you interested in? Is geographic territory or a remote position important? Perhaps culture, diversity, and inclusion are at the forefront when researching companies and industries that align with your goals.

If you are focusing on a particular industry or if you are changing industries, think about the types of companies you can look at, for example, nonprofit, private, government, or *Fortune* 100/500 companies.

Your answers to these questions will help you narrow your focus and become more productive in a short amount of time. Taking the approach of submitting your information to all positions that you may potentially qualify for will leave you submitting hundreds of resumes with little, if any, results. Take the time to set up your criteria on whatever job boards you decide to use, leaving out those that will not result in success. For those job boards you select, make sure you properly set up notifications, so you are notified of new postings.

If you have been conducting an active job search, you will need to refresh your online information — especially your resume and LinkedIn profile — every three to four weeks. Renewing your information increases your visibility to another set of recruiters and companies that did not see your information previously and now may see it when they post a new opportunity. If you do not refresh your information, you could be missed, or your information could be viewed as dated. Basically, refreshing your information moves you back to the front of the line.

Be vigilant, stay the course, and be patient. In this job market and depending on your specific skill set, it could take six months to identify, interview, and receive an offer for employment. Many job seekers are working job boards and talking to recruiters without getting anywhere. There are so many job seekers that I talk to daily who are frustrated, because they do not know where to turn or what to do next.

My advice is simple: *Have a plan and work the plan!* Step out of your comfort zone and take chances. It's your career, so take the steps necessary that others are either too afraid or too lazy to do. Reach out to higher-level connections at companies that interest you. Leverage your peers, alumni, networking groups, and more. It takes vigilance and in the end you WILL receive an offer for the right position with the right company at the right time!

CHAPTER 3
Your Resume and Cover Letter

YOUR RESUME IS AN IMPORTANT TOOL as you navigate the hiring process. But it is just a tool. Even though I don't consider the resume to be the most important part of finding the right position, I am addressing it as Chapter 3 because — to begin the networking process, create a LinkedIn profile, or even be considered for any position — your resume needs to be prepared in anticipation of your new career and position.

A while ago I signed up for a service that would refer potential clients to my Career Coaching business. Surprisingly, I was inundated with over 100 requests each day! Yet more interesting was that over 90 percent of the requests were for a resume writer. It was quite shocking that all these job seekers were looking for their first position or a new position, and their interest was only in having a "great" resume. Of course, you need a great resume, but it is not the most important component to find the right position. The responses inspired me to write a blog article ...

It's not just the resume!

As a Career, Executive, and Business Coach, I recently registered with LinkedIn's ProFinder service. Surprisingly, I am receiving over 100 notifications each day from LinkedIn members who are looking for coaching — and that's just local to Southern California. As a sole proprietor, it is impossible for me to personalize each response.

More than 90 percent of the requests are asking for someone to write or update their resume. Folks, resumes are a tool to get you to the next level in your job search. They will not secure a position for you or negotiate your salary — a resume is simply a tool that will generate interest by a potential employer about your background. In the last fifteen years the hiring process has dramatically changed. In order to navigate today's job search, you need to understand the nuances associated with the entire hiring process: networking, interviewing, negotiating — and yes a resume.

Having someone else write your resume takes away your personal touch, which is needed when applying for a new position. Further, someone else's writing can become confusing when sitting for an interview. My method is quite simple: follow my template, and I will assist you in editing the words and structure of your resume. By doing this, you will be comfortable with what you have written, and when you are sitting in front of a potential employer, you can be confident that what is on your resume is what you wrote.

Recently, a family member asked me to review a resume that was written by a professional resume writer who charged him substantially for this service. He asked what I thought of the resume, and I told him without hesitation that this resume did not capture the essence of what he did — plus I added that I could not understand exactly what he did.

I tell this story, because it captures the pitfalls of having someone else describe what you have done and what you can do for an employer! Can you be comfortable talking about your resume when sitting in front of a potential employer? Does your resume capture the essence of who you are, what you do, how you do it, and what you can do for the employer?

Remember, the resume is only a part of what is necessary to secure the position that is right for you. I have spent my life in some way or another as a Career Coach. Finding the right position for you is not only about having a "great" resume — it is the whole process of navigating the hiring process.

A resume is an important part of getting a position, but it is not the most important component you will need to find and decide on the right career and the right company.

Resume Tips

Have you sent out five, ten, fifty, or more resumes and have not received any responses? As a Career Coach this is perhaps the most often repeated phrase I hear when clients discuss their frustration in submitting resumes to potential employers. Countless times I have had clients say to me that they have sent out hundreds of resumes and have yet to receive a response. Finding the right career or position is not just about sending a resume. There are many components of your career search — a properly prepared resume is just one of them.

Your resume is a tool that is used to get you an interview. It will not get you a job. It will only detail and outline your experience to a potential employer. Years ago as a staffing recruiter and business owner, I worked with some companies that would hire employees just by reviewing a resume. They would let me know what skill set they were looking for, and I would have the employee just show up for the job. The hiring process has changed dramatically. Your resume offers only a small window to your ability to do the job and fit into the corporate culture.

Recently, I worked with a client who had been an elementary school teacher for over ten years. She wanted to make a career transition and, after a few coaching sessions with me, she decided to pursue a career in human resources. I helped her create a resume that showed her background as a teacher as well as how her interaction with her students and peers made her a perfect candidate for a position in human resources.

By applying the unique networking techniques discussed in the networking chapter, she was able to secure an interview with a major software company. She was told that she would undergo five interviews before being considered for acceptance. She had four successful interviews and was scheduled to speak with the regional manager. Unfortunately, this interview did not go well, and she was rejected for the position. While her resume did not show the specific experience the company required, it nevertheless got her an interview. Her rejection was not based on her resume nor on her ability to communicate her passions but only on one person's feelings — and that was out of her control. We will discuss interview techniques and how to handle those situations you can control and those you cannot control in the interviewing chapter.

Years ago, employers were interested mostly in your ability to perform the tasks of the position. There was little, if any, consideration of your soft skills (behavioral skills). But the hiring process has changed! Perhaps the biggest change is that previously 80 percent (a good guess) of the hiring decision was based upon your ability to do the job. Over the past twenty years or so, the hiring decision has evolved, so it is now a strong mix of your technical ability and your perceived and actual behavior.

With the onset of social media, companies will look at your LinkedIn profile, Facebook page, Twitter account, and so forth before they consider making you an offer. As you will see in the networking chapter, make sure you privatize and scour all of your social media accounts. Your resume then is only part of the process, yet it needs to let employers know who you are, what you do, how you do it, and what you can do for them.

Further, if you follow the steps and processes detailed in the networking chapter, your resume will be a validation of your networking conversations. Once you have networked into a company you have chosen and have had numerous conversations regarding your background and how you can be an asset to the company, your resume will simply be a reminder of your networking conversations. Simply said, the employer will already know who you are when they receive your resume for consideration.

Twenty professional coaches or resume writers will give you twenty different opinions and ideas regarding how to prepare and format your resume. And speaking candidly, all twenty are right! There is no perfect way to write a resume. Recruiters and hiring managers who are reviewing the resume will have differing opinions about what they want to see about the candidate they are considering hiring.

So you might ask: "Then why follow the advice in this chapter?" The answer is simple, as I have developed a template that considers everything you have accomplished coupled with your passions for your chosen career, so your resume will be attractive and professional — and it will be read.

Furthermore, we want to take the fluff out of the resume. By fluff I mean this: colors are not necessary, pictures of what you do are not necessary, and your picture on the resume is definitely a non-starter. Over the past few years it has become acceptable to place a company logo next to the name of the company you worked at. Your resume is a concentrated description of your experience and background and should not exceed two pages. Your resume needs to be concise, easy to read and attractive to the eye of the person reviewing your background. Practicing word parsimony (using as few words as possible to describe your experience) will allow the people reviewing your resume to see how you can be an asset to their organization.

Before we get started, let me make a few comments about your resume. As I mentioned, I am a firm believer in word parsimony, that is, say as much as you can with as few words as possible. As we will discuss in our chapter on recruiters, you will see how writing powerful descriptions in just a few words will attract their attention.

Also, you should not write anything on your resume that will disqualify you for the next step. For example:

- Listing hobbies or interests may disqualify you. Perhaps this can be best summed up with an imaginative example: If you were to say that your hobby is playing golf and the person reviewing your resume got hit in the head with a golf ball over the weekend, he or she may not be interested in speaking with you.

- In the Header of the resume, there is no need to list your street address. It is sufficient just to list the town you live in with your ZIP Code. In today's digital marketplace there is no need to let anyone know your exact address — safety first! Once you receive an offer, you will be asked for your mailing or residency address.

- Use a professional email address, for example, YourName@ Something.com. Using a cute email address is discouraged, for example, MyDogsName@Something.com.

- There is no need to write: "References will be furnished upon request." First, most companies will conduct reference checks once you have been selected for a position and, second, word parsimony!

There is no need to add words that do not have relevance. By using one more line to note your references you a taking up space that could be used to discuss your relevant experience.

- There is no need to include references on your resume or as an attachment (unless you have been asked to supply references). First, if you voluntarily list your references with a telephone number you might be very surprised that these references will be called. In the past I have provided reference names without notifying them I was using them as a reference, and they became a bit negative with the onslaught of calls. Second, make sure that any reference you list is a good reference. I know I don't have to mention this, but always select those references who will give you a positive referral and ask their permission to use them as a reference.

- Listing your education without dates is recommended. In many cases listing the year you graduated from college will give the potential employer an idea of your age. I would like to say that we are beyond the point of age discrimination just like I'd like to say that every time you send a resume someone will read it in its entirety — neither statement is true!

Using words such as *professional, highly motivated,* and *hardworking* go against the core of word parsimony! Consider that most employers are expecting you to be professional, highly motivated, and hardworking. There is no need to tell them what they already expect.

Types of Resumes

There are four distinct types of resumes:

1. Chronological
2. Functional
3. Chronological and functional combined
4. Government resume

I am not a fan of functional resumes and suggest you submit this type of resume to a potential employer only upon request. A functional resume consists of a series of bullet points discussing all the work you have done, your accomplishments, and the specific tools you have used in your previous positions. Further, it lists where and when you have worked without any job descriptions — just company names and dates of employment. And finally your education is listed. This book will not discuss the functional resume.

Government resumes are those that you submit to federal, state, county, and city agencies and government contractors; these are a breed among themselves and will not be discussed in this book.

Chronological resumes list each position you have had (including your current position), stating your most recent position first. Under each job description you are listing the work you have done, your duties and responsibilities, and your accomplishments. This is the easiest resume format to read, but it does not allow the people reviewing your resume to see the depth of your experience in the time they have allotted to read your resume. The only component missing from the chronological resume is the Experience Summary, which is the most useful component of the functional resume. Without the Experience Summary you are hoping that the people reviewing your resume will read all that you have accomplished in each position. The Experience Summary is a visual synopsis that allows reviewers to see your area of expertise and what you have accomplished in the first forty-five seconds of their review.

Based on my decades of experience, the type of resume I recommend is chronological and functional combined. This resume format is primarily based on the commonly used, easy-to-read chronological resume and features the useful Executive Summary from the functional resume. You'll see a detailed template in the following pages.

However, before we discuss specific formatting for your resume it is necessary to understand who is reviewing your experience. Please note that the hiring process for most companies is a necessity and not a priority. I cannot tell you how many times employers have called me to say they need someone or a group of employees to start "next week" only to have the hiring process delayed by several weeks. Don't get me wrong, hiring is important and necessary for all companies to grow. Yet when faced with the decision to hire a new employee or complete a project, the latter will prevail. Of course, companies will set high priorities for critical positions. Yet only a small percentage of hiring is for urgent positions.

If a recruiter, sourcer, screener, director, or manager is reviewing your resume along with other resumes (perhaps as many as fifty) you want to make sure you attract this person's attention. Simply stated, you have approximately fifteen lines of text and forty-five seconds to be considered for any potential next step in the hiring process. That is why you don't want to use the words noted above (professional, motivated, and so forth) or describe yourself as a workaholic. Interestingly, when I used to interview candidates and they told me they were workaholics, I would almost immediately end the interview. It's my feeling that if you have to tell me how hard you work then there may be some issues at play. Now fifteen lines may not seem like a lot of information, but you can easily sum up your experience and state the quality of your work by letting reviewers know:

- Who you are
- What you can do
- How you do it
- What you can do for the potential employer

There are hundreds of excellent and talented resume writers. There are also resume writers who have a hard time putting together a coherent sentence. If you are going to use a resume writer, review examples of his or her work and make sure your resume will represent the picture of you that you are trying to convey. I have seen some great work generated by resume writers, and I have seen resumes that were so nebulous you could not understand what was being said.

I urge you to make every attempt to write your own resume. If an outside service writes your resume, even from the notes you have given them, they are still not your words! During the interview it is sometimes difficult to talk about a resume that you have not written.

As noted previously, a relative used a resume writer and asked me what I thought about his resume. My first question was, "How much did you pay for this?" His answer dumbfounded me! Without revealing the amount, I can say he was taken advantage of! As I said before, the resume was vague and lacked a coherent description; I am sure few potential employers would consider him for a position with their company. He had applied for over a dozen positions without any response. After he allowed me to help him rewrite his resume, he was employed within a month.

Over the past few decades, I have seen candidates rejected for positions even though they were qualified for the position. In one case, I presented a mechanical designer's resume for a high-level position, and he was immediately rejected. His resume was well written, and all the experience required for the position was on his resume. The resume showed each position he had held with a good description of what he had accomplished and the specific tools he used. In this case, the employer was seeking a mechanical designer with over ten years of experience designing in a petrochemical environment. This mechanical designer worked for over twenty years at different petrochemical plants. His experience was a perfect match for this new position. Yet for the past eighteen months he had been working as a mechanical designer at a nuclear power plant. He was rejected, because the person reviewing his resume did not look past the first job! As mentioned above, a resume that uses the fifteen-line, forty-five-second rule will be noticed. If he had created a resume with an Experience Summary, he most probably would have been hired.

In another instance, I was conducting a series of recruiting training workshops. During the resume training session, I created a resume that was a perfect match for a position that I was working on for one of my staffing clients who often relied on me to find qualified candidates. On the second page, however — to make a point — I wrote: "Self-employed, homeless, and sold a variety of drugs." I submitted this resume to my staffing client (whom I knew well) for consideration. The company immediately requested an interview for this non-existent and questionable candidate! They never read the second page! This is a perfect example that a resume reviewer probably won't read the entire resume. (And I strongly suggest not trying this out!)

I cannot stress enough how important the first fifteen lines and forty-five seconds of your resume are — this is what will be reviewed and it's the key to moving on to an interview. After review of this first part of your resume, the reviewers — whether they have seen or not seen what they are looking for — will usually not continue reading the resume. There are too many resumes to review and not enough time. If you are qualified, you will most likely move to the next step in the hiring process where your resume will be read in its entirety. If you are considered not qualified, your resume will be set aside.

The template detailed in the following pages will allow you to create a resume that is attractive, on subject and, most importantly, readable. Follow this template to create a resume that will allow the person screening your resume to understand you are qualified and have the experience for the position. The goal is to attract the attention of the person reviewing your resume, so you will be considered for an interview.

I have created a resume template for the type of resume that is considered chronological and functional combined. Through my many years of experience in reviewing resumes coupled with discussions with senior human resource professionals, it is safe to say that your resume needs to express at least two important characteristics:

1. The person reviewing your resume needs to see in the first few lines: Who you are, What you do, How you do it, and What you can do for the potential employer. Remember, you only have up to fifteen lines and forty-five seconds to attract their attention.

2. As mentioned, many mid-size to large companies are using automated tracking system (ATS) software. Once you submit your resume to a company, it will undergo review by the automated system. The system has been programmed to find the keywords in the job description. If the keywords are missing from your resume, it will not be reviewed by a person, and it will be set aside. Make sure your resume includes the keywords — the most important words — stated in the job description. For example, if you are seeking a position as an accountant, keywords could include *accountant, accounting, budget, comptroller, controller, accounts payable/receivable,* and so forth. You can cut-and-paste the bullet points in your current Experience Summary, so the keywords show up in the first few bullet points of your resume and match those listed in the job description. Having the keywords will virtually ensure your resume will be reviewed in the next step of the process. For example, the Experience Summary in your current resume might present the key component of the job description listed as the third bullet point. In this case, it is a simple step to cut-and-paste the third line and make it the first bullet point.

You will see how the resume template below incorporates what is needed to attract the attention of an employer. There is no need to have two, three, or four different resumes, since you can rearrange (cut-and-paste) the bullet points on your resume to be in line with each job description.

The following resume template has five separate areas (depending on your skill set, background, and education). Each of these components will have an impact on how your resume is perceived. The template is designed specifically to attract the attention of the person reviewing your resume.

The first resume template version (below) includes an explanation of each section. The second version is a straightforward template, which you can copy and use when creating your own resume.

Resume Template With Explanations

HEADER

- Full name and titles — you want the employer to know immediately that you have, for example, an MBA or a PhD.

- Address: Your city, state, and ZIP Code are sufficient. In today's digital age, it is safer not to let everyone know exactly where you live.

- Telephone number: Use a number that is most convenient for you (cell phone or landline).

- Email address: Use an email address that is simple and not catchy! If you have an email address that you thought was cute at the time you created it, set up a new email address that is professional and simple. For example, YourName@Something.com is just fine.

- LinkedIn link: Go to your LinkedIn page, copy the link, and place it in the header.

EXPERIENCE SUMMARY

This is your key to being noticed! This part of your resume determines if the reviewer will continue to read the resume in its entirety. Remember, don't waste your words. Using words such as *professional, highly motivated,* and *hardworking* are unnecessary.

- It's important to note that this section is not simply a two-sentence summary. Instead, include up to fifteen bullet points to give reviewers the information necessary to review the rest of your resume. Each bullet point should be no more than two sentences in length.

- Your background and experience should be stated in words such as: Ten years of experience as an administrator, engineer, software designer, or paralegal (simply stating your skill set) with experience in your area of expertise.

- Each point should discuss your core competencies starting with the experience needed for the position. Remember you can always cut-and-paste bullet points to highlight the experience that is most relevant to a specific position. For example, if you are currently working as an administrator but have worked as a business analyst — and are hoping to land a new job as a business analyst — make sure the bullet point that discusses your business analyst background is the first bullet point.

- Attract the reviewer's attention by stating the work you have done that is specific to the position you are seeking.

- If you are transitioning to a completely different field, use the bullet points to describe your passion for the job. You can use work you have done to support your new career (for example, volunteer work and other activities that are similar). If you are looking to transition to a completely different career, this is where networking is the key to your transition.

- If this is your first position, use the bullet points to discuss how your background and education are a match for the position.

- If you are a Veteran of any branch of the U.S. military, the final bullet point should note that you have served (for example: United States Army Veteran).

EDUCATION

Noting your education just after the Experience Summary is a perfect way to let the potential employer know you have committed yourself to continued learning and have the educational experience needed for this position. It is important for a potential employer to see your educational accomplishments just after they have reviewed the Experience Summary, because this will give them an added incentive to continue reviewing your resume. List your education chronologically from the highest level down to your bachelor's degree. A PhD or master's degree should always come before your bachelor's degree. For example:

- University Name, Any Town, State, USA, MBA

- University Name, Any Town, State, USA, Bachelor of Science, your Major

If, however, your highest level of education was a high school diploma then you may choose to leave out this section and replace it with any certifications you have received that are relevant to the position. If you have not attended college you may put your education after the Experience section. In many instances you may not have a college education, but you have relevant life experience that qualifies you for the position. If this is the case you may want to consider adding additional bullet points to the Experience Summary, as this will in most cases get your resume forwarded to the next step in the process. Another point you can consider is extensive networking with the decision makers in the company in order to explain how your experience should outweigh the educational requirements.

EXPERIENCE

This part of your resume is designed to let the reviewer know where you have worked, what you have accomplished, and how long you have worked at the company. If you are a consultant and have numerous positions (performing the same tasks for different organizations) you can combine the experience instead of showing multiple job assignments in a two-to-five-year period. Numerous positions over a short period of time could possibly be a red flag to some employers.

It is important that you format the resume with consistency, so there is no confusion when the resume is being reviewed. If you are an employee and have had numerous positions in a short period of time, through no fault of your own — for example, a company's reduction in force (RIF) or job loss due to a merger or acquisition — list the companies where you worked and note the reason these employment times were limited.

Further, it is acceptable to have some redundancy in this section. You can repeat a few of the bullet points from the Experience Summary, but you might consider some minor rewording. Perhaps the best analogy in getting your experience noticed are the radio and television commercials that repeat a telephone number four or five times in just thirty seconds! They want you to remember a critical point. It is important to let your potential employer know the depth and breadth of your experience. Remember, those who are reviewing your resume are not reading every word — they are skimming your resume to quickly determine whether you might be a match. The format should be the same for each of your positions:

Company Name   *Date of Employment*

Position Title

- For each position, include up to five or six bullet points that describe the work you accomplished. (Again, there is no issue with repeating some of the bullet points and words from the Experience Summary.) Of course you can change the wording (or use the same wording), but by repeating your experience you are solidifying who you are and what you can do. If you worked as a contracted consultant or a contract worker, state the name of the company you were contracted to and completed the work for, not the name of the consulting firm.

- As noted earlier, gaps in employment can be a concern to a potential employer. By using phrases such as "work unrelated" or "caregiver for a family member," you can fill in the gaps and dates when you were not working in your area of expertise. If the gap is less than a year, you don't need to explain the time gap. If you are getting back into the job market after an extended absence, you will need to indicate what you were doing during this period.

- State all the companies where you have worked over the past ten years. There is no need to list the jobs you worked at over ten years ago. You can, however, list prior experience if the experience is relevant for the position you are considering. As an aside, during the onboarding process you may be asked to list all the positions you have had.

AWARDS AND CERTIFICATIONS

- If you have received awards from previous employers that are relevant to the position, you will list them here.

- If you have certifications that are not relevant to the position and you have not listed them in the Education section above, they can be listed here.

- As a reminder, do not list hobbies and interests, do not include your references, and do not state "references available upon request." It is safe to assume that once you receive an offer of employment you will be asked to furnish references, undergo a background check, and possibly undergo a drug screen.

Resume Template You Can Copy And Use

(HEADER)
FULL NAME, TITLE (if you have an advanced degree, e.g., PhD, MBA)
City, State, ZIP Code
Telephone Number
Email Address
Link to Your LinkedIn Profile

EXPERIENCE SUMMARY

- Include up to fifteen bullet points that describe your background and experience (one or two sentences per bullet point).

- Bullet points can be a duplicate of the bullet points used in the Experience section below.

- Bullet points can be interchanged to reflect the keywords in the job description.

- Don't use phrases such as *professional*, *highly motivated*, and *hardworking* — remember word parsimony!

EDUCATION

- List your education at this point in the resume if you have an advanced degree (for example, bachelor's degree, master's degree, or PhD). The reason for stating your advanced education here, early in the resume, is to show the employer that you have committed yourself to the experience needed for the position.

- List the name of the college or university, city, state, degree, and your major — do not reflect the years attended.

- List additional classes or certificates that are pertinent to your background and experience.

- If the position has no educational requirement and you don't have an advanced degree, then place Education at the end of the resume. Some positions do not have an educational requirement and not everyone looking for a new career, a career transition, or a new job has a degree. Not having a degree is not a negative and, in some instances, can be a plus for certain positions.

EXPERIENCE

- Company name, city, state, dates of employment — list your most recent job first.

- Do not list more than the last ten years of your experience. This will initially eliminate age discrimination and if, for example, your background is in a technical field the experience you had over ten years ago is not relevant.

- Each job description should be presented in bullet points and be easy to read — no more than ten bullet points per position.

- As noted previously, if you have a gap in your employment record, make sure that all dates and years are covered. You can include statements such as, "Unrelated work experience" or "Consultant." These statements can always be explained in the interview.

AWARDS AND CERTIFICATIONS

- Add awards and certifications that are relevant to the position. Note them here only if they are not noted above.

This resume template will be attractive to potential employers. It will give them an opportunity to see your background and experience at a glance. A skillfully crafted resume will move you to the next step — additional screening or the actual interview. Regardless of your experience, background, and specific expertise, you will not be noticed if your resume does not clearly state: Who you are, What you do, How you do it, and What you can do for the employer!

Let's briefly recap this section, so you can prepare an attractive resume:

- Your resume is a tool to get you noticed and a tool that will get you to the interview stage of the hiring process. Your resume will not get you a job, but without an attractive resume you have virtually little chance of securing an interview.

- It is critical to highlight your experience in the Experience Summary portion of the resume, since this part of your resume will attract the attention of a potential employer.

- Using unnecessary words can cause someone who is reviewing your resume to become distracted and not see the depth and breadth of your background.

- Never put anything on your resume that is not true! Stating you can perform a task that you cannot *will* come back to haunt you. This is not to say that you can't accentuate or highlight some part of your experience. If, for example, you have a background in software and the requirements ask for expertise in a specific program, you can (if in fact you do) state that you are familiar with the program. Or perhaps the requirements ask for two-plus years of working with a certain system, and you have worked with a similar system; you can state the similarities between the two systems.

- The Experience Summary should always state Who you are, What you do, How you do it, and What you can do for the company.

- The keywords in the job description should always be the first bullet points of the Experience Summary. This is the beauty of the Experience Summary. For every position, you can cut-and-paste the bullet points listed in the Summary to match the needs of the specific position. There is no need to have two or three different resumes!

- Use word parsimony to say as much as you can with the fewest number of words.

- A two-page resume is sufficient. Once you get to three pages or more, I can assure you that most employers will not read past the second page.

- It is not necessary to list your experience beyond the past ten years. On the one hand, if you are technical, I am sure the state-of-the-art technology from ten-plus years ago is outdated. In some cases, however, and based upon the requirements you may let the employer know in the interview that you have been performing these tasks for a long period of time. It is your subjective decision to discuss your entire experience and should only be made if you have knowledge of the company, the company culture, and the position requirement.

Cover Letters

Let me begin by saying that I am not a huge fan of cover letters. I cannot think of anyone who was hired because they composed a great cover letter. Sometimes cover letters are required and necessary. The cover letter is essentially a tease to get the employer to want to review your resume. By volunteering to write and include a cover letter with your resume you could risk disqualification even before an employer reviews your resume! I suggest that if a cover letter is not an additional requirement of your resume submission, don't write one!

If you feel you must write a cover letter — or you are asked to submit your resume with a cover letter — make sure that both your cover letter and your resume are in one document. In today's job market you want to make it easy for anyone to review your background and experience. By submitting separate documents you are asking the employer or recruiter to open your cover letter and then open your resume as separate documents.

The following paragraphs discuss the three main types of cover letters:

1. ***You feel you need to write a cover letter*** — If you are absolutely convinced you need to include a cover letter with your resume, it is time to rethink why you are writing it. Do you want to impress the company with your interest and your background? The resume does that for you. Do you want to let the company know you are qualified and ready for work? The resume does that for you. Is there some information that you have left out of your resume and you want to

include it in your cover letter? Then add that information to your resume. The main reason the voluntary cover letter is not necessary is simply because you could possibly use a phrase or make a statement that could disqualify you before the company has a chance to review your qualifications in your resume. You could be the most qualified candidate for a position, but your resume might never be reviewed because of a phrase or statement you made in the cover letter. If you still feel the need to include a cover letter with your resume, say as little as possible and just state your interest in the position. Use the cover letter as a tease to make them want to review your resume. You are submitting your resume for a position for which you are qualified. Your cover letter should only make them want to read about your background and experience. A sample voluntary cover letter should read:

———————————————————

Your Name
Your Address

Name of Company
Address
Attention: (Name)

Subject: Position #_____ Resume of (your name)

Dear (Name):

I am pleased to submit the attached resume for your consideration for the above referenced position.

I have researched (company name) and have targeted your organization as the company for which I would like to work. My background and qualifications are a perfect match for (position name). I am confident that I can be an asset to your organization.

I am looking forward to our next steps and meeting you to discuss (position name).

Please contact me at your earliest convenience to set a day and time to have a conversation.

Regards,
Your typed name or signature

---

2. ***The company has requested that you include a cover letter with your resume*** — A requested cover letter needs to follow the directions you are given by the potential employer. For example, if they ask you to describe your experience specifically or if they want to know how much experience you have that relates to their requirements, state the answers with just enough information to attract their attention. Don't restate everything in your resume, as this could be a red flag to the employer and your resume might not be reviewed. Again, make sure your resume and cover letter are combined as one document. Say just enough to gain their interest, so they will scroll down and review your resume. I remember years ago when I applied for a position with a company, they asked for a cover letter that would show how creative I was. In this instance the company was looking for a specific kind of creativity, and my response was a guess. This is why we stress the importance of networking. If I had spoken with

someone at the company before sending in my resume and cover letter, I would have had a good idea of what they were looking for. Suffice to say, my "creative guess" missed the mark, and I was never called for an interview.

3. *A government cover letter* — This cover letter usually includes everything that is on your resume plus an overview of just about everything you have ever done, how much you were paid, and how many hours you worked each week. To this day I cannot figure out the reason for the obvious redundancies, but I am sure the government processes are set up to create a workflow that is satisfying to this bureaucratic giant. We will not spend additional time discussing government cover letters.

Remember, a cover letter should simply be a tease to a potential employer to get them to look at your resume. If this introductory note becomes too technical and too redundant, there is an increased chance that you will disqualify yourself from consideration. If the cover letter is voluntary, just introduce yourself and let them know you are qualified for the position. If they ask for a cover letter, make sure you stay on subject and say just enough to entice them to review your resume.

CHAPTER 4

Online Job Boards and Company Websites

SEEKING EMPLOYMENT HAS BECOME AN ARTFORM. And getting your information seen by the right person is an entirely different playing field altogether. The go-to method for the typical job seeker is using online job boards. There are hundreds of specific job boards designed for each area of professional expertise. For example, there are nonprofit, government, sales, start-up, and executive sites, to name a few.

For now, let us discuss the most popular, go-to job boards for most job seekers. These include CareerBuilder, Indeed, Monster, Dice, ZipRecruiter and, of course, let us not forget about LinkedIn. If you ask most people in search of a job how they are getting their information out to prospective employers, they will most likely respond that they are using an online job board.

Online job boards are essential to enhance today's job search. They are the "enhancer not the answer." They should not and cannot be the only means of getting your name in front of a company, a hiring manager, or a recruiter. Most often and depending upon how well your resume is written, job boards and company websites rely heavily on applicant tracking systems (ATS). As mentioned previously, these systems weed out those resumes that are not qualified for the position by scanning the resume for keywords from the job description. These systems collect and sort through thousands of resumes to find the handful of candidates that best match the job description.

Whether anyone ever sees your resume could depend upon how well your resume is formatted with keywords for the ATS algorithms and ranking parameters established by the companies that use them. Many companies today have systems that are outdated, again causing your resume to fall into the black abyss with hundreds, if not thousands, of other potentially qualified candidates. I cannot tell you how many times a client has come to me and said that they have sent out hundreds of resumes and are still waiting for a response.

In my opinion, there is a lot of work left to do in perfecting the ATS systems, as I know many qualified job seekers who would be a perfect match for a position and never receive a call or hear from a company after they submit their resume. I have found over the last eight-plus years that the way you format your resume is essential. It's also essential to use keywords that these systems are programmed to identify based on the job description.

I am sure you have noticed when submitting your resume (uploading it) to a job posting that your information gets distorted. The ATS algorithms are deciphering if you are worthy of a resume review or telephone call from a recruiter. Or perhaps you are familiar with the standard email response you receive about twenty seconds after you have submitted your resume. More often than not, you will never hear from the company again or be provided the respect of a personal response. So you wait and hope for a call. How do you even know at this point who to follow up with? Does your resume really represent who you are and how ABC company can benefit from your expertise? As I mentioned, many highly qualified job seekers fall to the bottom of the resume stack.

There are several resources out there to help you optimize your resume based on a specific job description. Jobscan, for example, can assist you in preparing your resume for an ATS review. This platform allows you to upload your resume along with a job description, and it provides a quick analysis to see how well your resume aligns with that position's description. The program will indicate areas that need to be enhanced, so you can become a top candidate for consideration. There is a free version that allows you to scan your current resume and a job description. With the subscription version, you can perform multiple scans to see your "match rate." The program provides recommendations on the enhancements you should make to get your resume recognized by the employer. Just taking this small step will increase your odds for engagement exponentially.

Each and every time you submit your resume to a job posting you MUST tailor your resume — EVERY SINGLE TIME without exception! Remember in the chapter on resumes you learned about the Experience Summary? You can interchange the bullet points in the summary, so the most applicable skill set is the first point scanned by the ATS. Or you can add one or two bullet points with the appropriate keywords. For example, if your first bullet point in the Experience Summary discusses your project management experience and the company is seeking someone with organizational management background, you can easily cut-and-paste the two bullet points in your resume, so your organizational management experience is the first bullet point.

When to Use an Online Job Board

You may have used job boards and company websites to apply for a position. You may have submitted a resume and, even though you felt you were perfect for the position, you received either no response from the company or one of those pre-written letters letting you know you are not qualified for the position. Online job boards and company websites are great tools, but they are not perfect. They are not perfect because, although you may be qualified, the ATS sees you as a submittal and not a person. We will discuss how to make a resume submittal more personal in the networking chapter.

Of course you can use a job board or a company website to discover a variety of jobs that are available or a position that may be open at one of the companies you have chosen. There are four possible reasons that you may not receive a response after you submit your resume:

1. ***You did not read the job description, and you are not qualified*** —
You may have signed up with a job board and your resume is auto-matically submitted for a job opening that matches your keywords. As mentioned previously, in some cases the technology has not caught up with the concept. One word on your resume that resem-bles a part of the job description could have your resume in front of a potential employer even though you are not even remotely qualified for the position. This situation is not in your control. Once you see a position title that is in line with your experience and background, make sure you take time to read the job description. You might see the job title and feel you are qualified for the position. Then almost immediately you receive a stock note letting you know you are not qualified. Reading the entire job description is both for your benefit and the benefit of the company — no one's time is wasted. A few years ago I was helping a human resource manager in their recruit-ing efforts. This aerospace organization was looking for a customer service specialist. We posted the position on a major job board with a specific job description. We also listed the position as "Customer Service Representative — Aerospace." In just twenty-four hours I received over 300 resumes! And only ten were qualified! Every other resume was from a customer service person who had worked in a restaurant or department store or had a customer service position at a company that was completely unrelated to the aerospace indus-try. None of these candidates took time to read the job description! Before you send or submit your resume for a position — READ THE JOB DESCRIPTION.

2. ***The position may have been filled*** — If this is the case, the company may not have updated their job board or website to remove the posting.

3. *The company may be testing the job market, because it may have a position open in the future or have a project that is not anticipated to begin for months* — They are collecting (ghosting) resumes and wasting your time. Unfortunately, there is no way of knowing if they are collecting resumes for a position that is months away. In many cases if you do not receive a response within ten working days from the time you submitted your resume, you can assume the company is probably collecting resumes.

4. *Some larger companies may have a policy to first hire from within the company but are required to interview candidates from outside the company* — Be very careful of this situation, because the odds may be stacked against you. When you are asked for an interview you can always ask if there is an internal candidate being considered for the position.

Using online job boards and company websites to find a position is only part of the process. Granted, if you have a critical skill set (for example, a respiratory therapist during a pandemic), I am sure that using job boards and company websites will suffice. Yet for non-critical skill sets, you cannot completely rely on using just the job boards and company websites. You need to enhance your job search activities with assertive communication including networking; direct communication with the company, recruiter, or hiring manager; and tapping into other business and social media outlets.

Advice and Insight From Other Human Resource Professionals and Recruiters

Over the last four decades, we have developed long-term relationships with human resource managers, human resource generalists, and recruiters. As we developed the outline for this book, we reached out to a few of these contacts to ask for their opinions about job boards, company websites, and the hiring process in general. After contacting them with a list of questions, we received answers that were surprisingly quite different. The insight these professionals offer is worth its weight in gold!

Questions on Topic 1 – Technology

How have technological advancements in the past twenty years impacted your recruiting process? Responses regarding positive impacts:

- "Numerous ways to connect with candidates. Impact seen immediately." — Brandon D., Senior Contract Recruiter

- "Easier focus on 'buzz words' and skill sets. Speed in finding the right candidates is vastly increased." — Cornell H., Senior Contract Recruiter

- "Fast and more efficient." — Ann C., Director of Human Resources

- "Streamlined processes; added many new recruiting resources such as job search sites (for example, Indeed.com), added the use of mobile platforms that allow candidates to apply to jobs on their phones which, in turn, yields a larger applicant pool. The use of technology has also allowed us to virtually meet candidates via Skype and Zoom, which has opened territories substantially." — Valerie G., Corporate Recruiter

Responses regarding negative impacts:

- "Candidates become numb to outreach." — Brandon D., Senior Contract Recruiter

- "Sometimes I feel that technology has impersonalized the hiring process." — David M., Senior Corporate Recruiter

- "In many instances we miss qualified candidates, because our systems are not user friendly." — John H., Director Human Resources

Please discuss how your ATS is used for screening applicants:
- "An ATS is a great tool for managing your candidates that have applied to a specific role, but it also can be a great tool for building a pipeline for future roles. Depending on what ATS you use, you can build lists of candidates using specific codes or keywords so that you're able to search and find candidates who have previously showed interest in your company." — Valerie G., Corporate Recruiter

- "The more advanced ATS systems will screen out the candidates who are not qualified for a specific position. I have found it to be a great recruiting tool." — John H., Director Human Resources

Does the ATS hinder or enhance your hiring process?
- "It does a little of both; we are able to get the candidate through the system and hire them quickly, but these systems have a difficult time distinguishing candidates when doing a simple job search." — Brandon D., Senior Contract Recruiter

- "It actually depends on the specific tool the company has chosen. While ATS systems were developed to enhance the recruiting process some of them can be too cumbersome and have too many bells and whistles, which can add many unnecessary steps to the recruiting process." — Valerie G., Corporate Recruiter

- "In about one half of the requirements we find that we received candidates who are not even remotely qualified. The screening process may only find one word that is applicable to the job description. The technology does not screen out the candidates who cannot perform the job and it is time wasted." — Dan M., Vice President of Human Resources

Who determines the ranking parameters (human resources, talent acquisition, or the hiring manager)?

- "Talent acquisition and the hiring team." — Valerie G., Corporate Recruiter

- "Hiring managers and human resources." — Dan M., Vice President of Human Resources

- "Talent acquisition." — Madeline S., Manager of Talent Acquisition

- "The hiring managers." — John H., Director of Human Resources

Do you ever miss a qualified applicant due to the algorithms and ranking parameters set by your company?

- "Most probably. The applicant pool is so large that finding the most qualified candidates is almost impossible." — Brandon D., Senior Contract Recruiter

- "Sure, that's definitely possible." Valerie G., Corporate Recruiter

- "I am sure we have missed our share of qualified candidates, but I feel that we have also identified candidates that we could have never found without the parameters we have set." — George W., Director of Human Resources

- "We probably miss about 25 percent of the qualified applicants." — Cornell H., Senior Contract Recruiter

How do you control an applicant resume submission that is presented outside your ATS?

- "Enter them manually." — Valerie G., Corporate Recruiter

- "We usually do not consider the candidate." — John H., Director of Human Resources

- "If a candidate's resume is sent to anyone other than human resources, they are immediately disqualified." — George W., Director of Human Resources

In your opinion, where in the process does the ATS break down?

- "Lack of efficient documentation. Junk in/junk out." — Valerie G., Corporate Recruiter

- "Most ATS systems do not screen out the candidates who are not even remotely qualified." — John H., Director of Human Resources

- "Technology has not caught up to the concept!" — George W., Senior Director of Human Resources

Questions On Topic 2 – Hiring Process

What is your approximate cycle time to hire?

- "Industry average is about forty-five days from the date of requisition opening to the date of hire." — Valerie G., Corporate Recruiter

- "We try to have a maximum of thirty days in our cycle, but the average is approximately forty days." — John H., Director of Human Resources

- "Sixty days minimum!" — Susan R., Executive Vice President of Human Resources

- "We are a small business, and it can take as little as seven days from the time we interview them to the time they start working." — Lori Z., Administrative and Human Resource Manager

Once you identify a candidate, pre-screen, interview, and extend an offer of employment, how long is the onboarding process?
- "Our onboarding process is quite extensive, so it could take as much as six weeks." — John H., Director of Human Resources

- "We have completed the onboarding process in less than one week." — Lori Z., Administrative and Human Resource Manager

Please give you opinion on the "quick apply" feature? Can this feature disqualify qualified applicants?
- "Not aware of this feature." — Cornell H., Senior Contract Recruiter

- "I have seen this feature but never used it. I am positive that it could disqualify an applicant." — Bill R., Human Resources Manager

What percentage of the interview process is technical versus soft skills (behavioral)?
- "Approximately 60 percent soft skills and 40 percent technical skills for highly technical positions. Approximately 80 percent soft skills and 20 percent technical skills for non-technical roles." — Valerie G., Corporate Recruiter

- "It is a fifty/fifty split between technical skills and soft skills." — Ann C., Director of Human Resources

- "We have seen soft skills become more and more important over the past ten years. Today it is over 60 percent of our decision to hire." — Johanna C., Vice President of Human Resources

- "It's about 40 percent technical." — Brandon D., Senior Contract Recruiter

Do you have a set process for conducting behavioral interviews?
- "We have developed a test and a list of company-centric questions that will give us an idea of how the candidate with assimilate into our culture." — George W., Director of Human Resources

- "The behavioral interview is perhaps as important as the technical interview, so we have developed a process for these interviews." — Madeline S., Manager of Talent Acquisition

It has recently become standard practice for mid-size and large companies to conduct automated video interviews to pre-screen or to determine if a candidate is qualified. Can you explain why this process is effective or if this process is considered impersonal?
- "I find it impersonal as there is no interaction with the candidate." — Brandon D., Senior Contract Recruiter

- "This is a great tool for pre-screening candidates as the first step in the interview process as it allows the recruiter to take note of any non-verbal communication queues that you just can't pick up during a phone call." — Valerie G., Corporate Recruiter

Questions On Topic 3 – Cover Letters

Are cover letters helpful?
- "No. Applicant tracking systems use the last cover letter submitted. So the cover letter would need to change with every cover letter submitted." — Brandon D., Senior Contract Recruiter

- "Not often." — Cornell H., Senior Contract Recruiter

- "Yes, we read them religiously." — Ann C., Director of Human Resources

- "Some companies require cover letters as part of the process as a writing sample while other companies do not. As a recruiter, I scan them quickly before reviewing the attached resume. If I don't find what I'm looking for on the resume, then I'll go back to the cover letter to see if that specific skill is mentioned on the cover letter." — Valerie G., Corporate Recruiter

Does your human resource team read the cover letters?
- "No. With the amount of resumes we receive we feel that cover letters do not add any value." — John H., Director of Human Resources

- "Sometimes but rarely do they have any effect on whether or not we call the candidate for an interview." — Madeline S., Manager of Talent Acquisition

- "If we don't ask for a cover letter we don't read it. If we require a cover letter that outlines the candidate's experience, we will read the letter." — Lori Z., Administrative and Human Resource Manager

Can a cover letter disqualify an applicant from a position?

- "Yes. If there are errors or if it is poorly written this can lead to disqualification." — Valerie G., Corporate Recruiter

- "In many instances the candidates will give us too much information in the cover letter and more than 50 percent of the time the letter will cause immediate disqualification." — George W., Director of Human Resources

- "My advice is that if you are not asked to send a cover letter, don't!" — John H., Director Human Resources

Questions On Topic 4 – Applicant Feedback

Our feedback has revealed that oftentimes an applicant is ghosted by a recruiter — they are told they are the perfect candidate and will be moved to the next step in the hiring process, but weeks will pass without any communication. Can you explain why?

- "As a candidate, this is the most frustrating thing that can happen. It's happened to me several times, and it's maddening! The only reason I can think of why this would happen is if the position is cancelled or the hiring manager lacked follow-through with the recruiter (or anything along those lines — where the process wasn't moving forward any longer) and the recruiter doesn't have a definitive update/answer to relay to the candidate, so they choose to make no attempt to reach out to the candidate. In my opinion, they do this because they are not comfortable giving unfavorable news or admitting that the process has stalled. Giving bad news is never fun, but it needs to be done to close the loop. Personally, my practice is to call all active candidates (candidates who have interviewed for the position) when the position is filled and provide feedback. This is a good way to remain connected to your candidates for future opportunities and is an excellent company branding exercise." — Valerie G., Corporate Recruiter

- "The only time we don't have a timely response to a candidate is when we have multiple openings, but we try to get back to them as soon as possible." — Madeline S., Manager of Talent Acquisition

Some companies post "ghost" positions to increase their resume pipeline for a future position. Can you offer any validity to this claim?
- "That's not something I've ever taken part in during my years as a corporate recruiter." — Valerie G., Corporate Recruiter

- "I have never seen that happen, although I have heard that some companies make this a standard practice." — George W., Director of Human Resources

- "There have been only two instances in the past where we had an upcoming project, so we collected resumes in anticipation of the work that needed to be done." — David M., Senior Corporate Recruiter

If your company policy is to first consider an internal hire are you required to interview candidates who are not employed by your company? If so, do you let the applicant know that you have an internal candidate?
- "Yes, I let both parties (internal candidate and external candidate) know who's in the running." — Valerie G., Corporate Recruiter

- "Our company policy is to first consider internal candidates and, unfortunately, we also need to interview external candidates. We do not let the external candidates know about the possible internal hire until the end of the interview. I am trying to change this policy with the company as I know it wastes the time of the external candidates applying for the position." — John H., Director of Human Resources

Questions On Topic 5 – Resumes

What is the most important element of a resume?
- "The body of the resume: writing style, grammar, previous experience, specific skills, and finally, dates of employment." — Valerie G., Corporate Recruiter

- "The resume needs to get right to the point. By that I mean the resume needs to let us know that the candidate is qualified for the position. I have seen too many resumes that talk about everything but the candidate's qualifications. The resume needs to let us know they can do the job." — David M., Senior Corporate Recruiter

- "I have seen too many resumes that have not been spellchecked, and that is an immediate disqualifier. My suggestion to everyone is to have your resume read by someone else for edit." — Lori Z., Administrative and Human Resource Manager

What is your opinion of resumes that have a picture of the applicant, multiple colors, and different fonts?
- "I'm not a fan of the use of pictures. I don't mind different fonts or colors." — Valerie G., Corporate Recruiter

- "No pictures, graphs, colors, or anything that is cute to try to attract my attention. I am only interested in the candidate's qualifications." — George W., Director of Human Resources

- "If you send me a resume with a picture of yourself on it, I will trash it!" — Cornell H., Senior Contract Recruiter

Do you prefer a chronological or functional resume?
- "Both serve a purpose, but I prefer pre-screening with a chronological resume. It flows better." — Valerie G., Corporate Recruiter

- "I will only accept a chronological resume." — Madeline S., Manager of Talent Acquisition

- "We feel that a functional resume may have something to hide by not letting us know the specific work the candidate performed at each company." — John H., Director of Human Resources

(Note: As a reminder, the resume template presented in the previous chapter is a combined chronological and functional resume. By combining the chronological resume with the most useful part of the functional resume — the Experience Summary — you are allowing the resume reviewer to easily see your experience and accomplishments. Combining these two resume styles simply creates an enhanced chronological resume.)

How many pages can a resume be and still be acceptable?
- "No more than two pages unless it's a highly functional resume." — Valerie G., Corporate Recruiter

- "I have seen fifteen-page resumes and resumes that can't stretch to one page. Two or three pages at the most is acceptable." — Lori Z., Administrative and Human Resource Manager

- "Two pages maximum!" — Madeline S., Manager of Talent Acquisition

How many years of experience should be noted on a resume for mid-career and late-career candidates?
- "Ten years is ideal." — Valerie G., Corporate Recruiter

- "No more than ten years unless the experience is applicable to the position." — George W., Director of Human Resources

- "Fifteen years, tops!" — Cornell H., Senior Contract Recruiter

Questions On Topic 6 – Recruiting

Do your recruiters "direct recruit"? (Direct recruiting is when a recruiter will recruit from a company's competitor or approach a candidate who is currently working.)
- "Yes, I do." — Valerie G., Corporate Recruiter

- "Our recruiters work from both job boards and direct recruiting from any source possible including our competitors." — Lori Z., Administrative and Human Resource Manager

Do your recruiters recruit exclusively from job boards and company websites?
- "Not exclusively, no." — Valerie G., Corporate Recruiter

- "If we are recruiting for a very critical job skill we will spend time recruiting with every tool available including job boards, networking sites, and from other companies." — George W., Director Human Resources

———————————

Understanding the limits of submitting your resume through an online job board or company website is one of the keys to having your resume reviewed. Complete dependence on job boards and company websites will place you in that class of people who report: "I sent out 100 resumes and did not get a single response." Eventually technology will catch up with the concept and these Internet tools will be beneficial to both you and the employer. But for now, use these tools as a guide to research the companies you want to work for and the position you have chosen as your career.

The advice in this book, coupled with your research and networking, will empower you to find the right position with the right company. Recognizing that job boards and company websites are just a part of your job-search process is the perfect segue to the next chapter on networking.

CHAPTER 5
The Art of Networking

NETWORKING IS PERHAPS THE MOST IMPORTANT ELEMENT in finding the right position with the right company. The Art of Networking is your ability to research, identify, and connect with a contact who can help you learn about a company, find a mentor, or perhaps find the position you want. Connecting with the right person and communicating your interest in working for the company is the essence of networking. Networking will allow you to stand out from the other applicants who are sending in their resumes and passively waiting for a response.

Many applicants will submit their resumes through an online job board or company website without any additional follow up. Your networking efforts will allow you to be noticed, because you took the time to reach out to make a connection and possibly engage in a conversation about the company and a potential job.

As technology advances, so do networking sites. LinkedIn is a good example of a networking site, while also serving as an online job board. As I mentioned in the chapter on job boards, the technology has yet to catch up with the concept. This is also true with business networking sites, although they are much further advanced. The business networking sites are in a constant state of flux. You will notice that from one week to the next they may change their wording, layout, or navigation. Be flexible, because the results will be the same and the outcome of your networking effort will remain constant.

Networking is the key to finding the right position with the right company! The networking component of the hiring process is as important in securing a position with the company you have chosen as your resume and your interview. As you seek to find a company that is compatible with your career goals including the position, the company culture, and an environment that will enable you to grow and prosper throughout your career, proper networking will help you to know the choice you have made is the right one. Networking is an art form and, after making the initial contact, this is a perfect way to find the company and the position you want.

In years past, finding a position was usually accomplished by submitting a resume to an open position, securing an interview, and accepting a position. Oh how the process has changed! Finding an open position on a job board or a company's website and forwarding your resume for consideration usually finds your resume lost in a "black hole." How many times have you sent in a resume, knowing you were qualified for the position, and never got a response? Or you sent in a resume and almost immediately received a response that says, "Thank you for submitting your resume but, unfortunately, we have more qualified candidates." In my coaching career virtually hundreds of clients have told me that they have sent out over 200 resumes and never received a response.

To put it bluntly, the hiring process has become impersonal! That is not to say that companies do not care, but we are discussing the resume submittal and review process. Networking will allow you to take the impersonal aspect out of the process by connecting with the right people who can guide you through the company's hiring practices.

Earlier in this book I mentioned a former client — a project manager who worked for a consulting company that was contracted to the government. He engaged my services, because he was qualified and ready to move into program management. He wanted to transition from government contracting to health-care. And he was commuting to the East Coast each week and wanted to find a position closer to his West Coast home. Had he simply applied to a program management position in a healthcare organization, I am sure he would still be looking today. But through the magic of networking he was able to network with two or three companies and, in the end, he was offered a position as a program manager for a national healthcare organization.

What were his steps to success? First, he connected with four healthcare companies and their management teams. He was able to schedule telephone conversations with a few managers. He was referred to four other managers. Finally, he connected and spoke with a manager who was interested in his background. This manager became his champion and helped to create a position for my client. In the end, he was offered the position he wanted at the salary he expected. Networking works!

Networking is the key to understanding a position and the company and making sure that your background and experience are noticed by the employer you have chosen. The relationships you create through network-ing can help you find a mentor or a company champion — or even create a position that did not exist.

In-Person Networking

Developing internal and external relationships is key to getting your name and professional qualifications to a potential employer. There are opportunities to make a significant number of connections through in-per-son interactions at professional associations, conferences, workshops, trade-shows, Meetup groups, chambers of commerce, and more.

There are a wide variety of ways in which like-minded professionals can connect in person. For decades, networking at professional association meetings and conferences has been the gold standard to meet other profes-sionals in your field (or your newly chosen field). For example, if you are a woman working in technology, consider joining Women in Technology International. If you are a woman who works in the retail industry, you would reach out to Women in Retail. If you are a human resources professional, you can connect with the Society for Human Resource Management.

Another way to connect with other professionals is to mentor small business owners who need professional guidance through Score.org. And, of course, you can look into regional Meetup groups. These are just a few of the hundreds of resources available to job seekers. All it takes is a little research to find the organizations that best support your goals. Be bold! When it comes to networking, making the effort to meet other professionals in person simply can't be beat.

Virtual Networking

In addition to in-person networking opportunities, you can also network virtually. As a job seeker in today's job market your digital presence matters! These days, digital marketing is how job seekers connect with peers, customers, and like-minded professionals. Yet if you are like most people this can be daunting, depending on how comfortable you feel with social media. The twenty-first century is a virtual society, and it is only going to increase in the months and years ahead. Depending upon your generation and how comfortable you are with technology and social media, networking virtually may greatly impact your success. Many job seekers struggle with just how to effectively reach out and make virtual connections. They wonder: Who do I connect with? How do I connect? What do I say?

To begin your networking process, we must remember what you are trying to accomplish. You must be highly focused, as networking and looking for a position are rightly considered a full-time job! Understanding the networking process and using it to your advantage allows you to brand yourself, so you can get the job you want.

If you are looking to expand your network, it's helpful to remember that other job seekers, companies, and their employees need to continually expand and increase their online visibility. I talk to hundreds of job seekers monthly, and I hear the same thing from mid-level managers to C-level executives (for example, CEO, CFO, and CIO) and board members: "I've never had to network before or even think about building my professional network via LinkedIn or any other platform." In past years many employees have had the luxury of leaving one position having already secured another. Times have changed!

So how do you begin building your network? What do you say and how do you say it? My advice is to keep it simple. Do not let LinkedIn or any other virtual networking outlet intimidate you. Now more than ever employers and their decision makers are open to making connections with professionals inside and outside of their industry. They understand the importance of broadening their own professional network. By doing this you are connecting with people outside or inside your industry, and that helps to create a broader sphere of connections and influencers. This is particularly important if you are thinking about changing your industry vertical or transitioning your career, or if your industry has been greatly impacted by social or economic turmoil (the COVID-19 pandemic is a good example). In this case, making a shift in your mindset and looking into another industry is needed. Expanding your network is critical, and so is the way you work on expanding it.

Ask yourself what your professional interests are and if you can leverage your professional accomplishments in a different industry. Use LinkedIn to conduct research into industries, companies, and contacts. Connecting with human resources and recruiting personnel is discouraged (unless of course you are a human resource professional) as the first connection at a company. In many instances, you will find that this connection will simply result in a request to submit your resume for consideration with the other several hundred interested applicants. If however you connect first with a manager or director at a company and they immediately refer you to human resources you can now reach out to human resources with a referral from the person who suggested you speak with HR (when asked to contact human resources don't forget to get the name of the HR representative). Having a referral to HR can become a first step in having your resume reviewed.

A key to your networking success is to connect with the C-level executives, directors, and managers. By doing this you can discover almost everything you need to know about the company. By using LinkedIn and other business networking platforms, you can identify the managers or directors with whom you want to connect. Once the connection is made, there is a window of opportunity to provide engaging and meaningful content to your new connection, especially if there is an opening that meets your professional criteria. Throw your hat into the ring. What do you have to lose? Be bold, be different, but most importantly be genuine in your approach. Further, I cannot tell you how many of my clients have networked with company executives and managers who were able to create a new position that matches their background and experience.

Once you have connected with a director or manager at a company and you have had a positive dialog, send an additional note requesting a time to have a conversation to learn more about the organization. Although it will be inferred that this is a call about employment, your conversation should center around your research of the company.

Starting the discussion by asking questions about the company culture, the size of the department, and their management style will show the manager or director that you are completing your research in order to make the correct decision about the company with whom you would like to work. For example, "Thank you for connecting with me on LinkedIn. I have researched your company, and I would like to learn more about the organization."

Once the conversation takes on a positive tone you can now segue the discussion to your job search. For example, you could say, "This sounds like a great organization. Who should I speak with about a future opportunity?" My experience has shown that you will receive one of four responses:

- "I am the person you should be talking to."

- "You will need to speak with John, as he is the manager of the department."

- "You will need to speak with Georgia in human resources."

- "We are not hiring right now."

With the first response you can now talk about your background and how you can be an asset to the organization. With the second and third responses you now have a referral to another contact within the company. By having a "network referral" your networking becomes a much simpler task, and you are growing your sphere of influence within the company.

If however you are told that they are not hiring at this time keep in mind that hiring is cyclical. Let the contact know that you would like to stay in touch as you are quite interested in working for the company. Many of my coaching clients have been told that there are no current open jobs only to find that within a couple of weeks they receive notice that a position has opened, and the manager has reached out to them. Keeping your name in front of a potential employer is another key to successful networking.

Tips to Use LinkedIn's Robust Capabilities

In the eyes of most employers, recruiters, and job seekers, LinkedIn is the most reputable resource out there. Therefore, let's focus on this hardworking job-search and networking tool. First, making sure your profile tells your professional story is key to your success. Make sure your current profile highlights enough about you to capture a future employer's interest. Better yet, if you were an employer looking to hire someone with your experience would you make a connection based on your current profile? If you are wavering in your response to the question, your profile needs a little work.

The smallest tweaks can make the biggest impact in terms of how you are viewed by a potential employer. If your profile is put together haphazardly and does not give a level of detail about who you are and your experience, odds are a future employer will pass.

Take the time to represent yourself well. How you present yourself via LinkedIn will influence how a future employer may view you and your ability to perform at the highest level. A little attention to detail goes a long way. If you do not take time in the beginning to properly set yourself up on LinkedIn and take advantage of all that LinkedIn has to offer, you will miss out on some golden opportunities.

If you are actively seeking a job, we highly recommend that you purchase LinkedIn Premium. Don't get me wrong, the free version of LinkedIn is beneficial, but there are expanded features in the Premium level that will help in your job pursuit. One of the biggest features is the ability to connect with people who are viewing your profile. They are often recruiters, talent acquisition personnel, or human resource professionals conducting a keyword search for skills that brought them to your profile.

Have you received a notification when logging into LinkedIn that someone has looked at your profile only to see this was an anonymous view? If you have either a free or Premium account, you will not be able to see anyone who has viewed your profile while they are in a private mode. Usually those who choose the private mode are recruiters and business professionals who are browsing profiles in private mode to find candidates, sales leads, potential clients, or business partners.

For those people who are not in the private mode who have reviewed your profile, you will be able to view a list of these people's names. You should send a note or a connection request. An example of a note to someone who has viewed your profile could read, "Susan, I noticed you reviewed my profile. I am always looking to expand my network, let's get connected professionally through LinkedIn." Or "Susan, I noticed you reviewed my profile. Was there something about my experience that interested you? I'm always looking to expand my network inside and outside of my industry. Let's get connected." These are just a few ways to begin a dialogue — and remember, keep it simple.

There seems to be some confusion on where and how to connect. On a LinkedIn profile you can set up security measures. These privacy and security tabs offer several ways to connect with the person you have identified as a key contact at the company. You will see on their profile a couple of different tabs or icons that will allow you to send them a message. There will be a connect tab (great, send a message), or perhaps you will see a message tab that has a lock on it. Unless you have Premium capabilities, you will not be able to InMail this person, however, you can click on the "three dots" or the "more tab" (located just under the profile and picture) that provide several options to connect and send them a personal message. Or save their profile to a PDF and follow them.

Remember to refresh your brand — your LinkedIn profile tells your professional story. It speaks to your personality, professional milestones, and accomplishments. It also helps you stand out on LinkedIn to recruiters, future employers, and a prospective client. LinkedIn provides background photos from which you can choose an appropriate picture. Choose one that resonates with you and your personality.

Here are a few easy instructions to begin enhancing your profile. Please note that your LinkedIn screens may differ depending upon whether you have a free LinkedIn account or Premium account (see Figures 1 and 2):

1. Click the Me icon at the top of your LinkedIn home page.

2. Click View Profile.

3. Click on the background photo and choose one of the following options:

- Upload a photograph.
- Select an image from the LinkedIn library of images.
  - Reposition to drag and reposition the image (options available on the image itself).
  - Delete photo to remove the image.
  - Change photo to change the current background photo (scroll down the page to see the imagery options) or upload your own professional image.

Here are some ideas to consider when choosing a background photo:

- Select a photo or quote that captures your personality.

- Add a photo that captures a memorable moment with your work team.

- Choose a photo that highlights a special milestone in your career such as receiving an award.

- Learn more about making your photo look more professional with LinkedIn filters and how you can add or change your background photo.

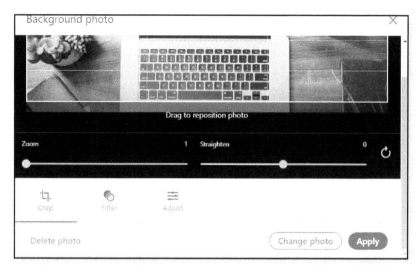

Figure 1.

Figure 2.

Completing your profile increases your visibility. And enhancing your profile is more likely to increase interest with potential employers. This important act will lead to increased interest. Here are just a few suggestions to reignite a stale profile:

- Update your photo (no dogs, cats, family photos of your spouse and kids, or vacation shots of you and your spouse frolicking on the beach). Remember, LinkedIn is a professional site.

- Leave your personal photo album for Facebook and Instagram! In fact, let us talk about other social media outlets for a moment — clean them up! If you post anything political or anything you would not want your family members to see, delete it or archive it, especially while you are being considered for future employment. Future employers do research, and you should too! Privatize your social media accounts — this will ensure that no one can post to your accounts who is unknown to you and you can chose who can view your information.

Begin following influencers that post messages that resonate with you, comment on their post, and repost their message. (To locate an influencer who could assist you in your networking and making networking connections, just go to the Search section in the upper-left corner and search for *influencers*.) If you feel comfortable writing on a specific topic of interest with respect to your professional area of expertise then, by all means, develop content such as blog posts. Beginning to blog will increase your visibility, will enable you to showcase and share your expertise, and will allow you to gain followers.

When you decide to send a connection message to a fellow LinkedIn member, read his or her profile and look for commonalities such as location, education, position, shared connections, and hobbies. Perhaps reference the person's recent blog or posting. Ask to connect. Believe it or not, future employers look to see how connected you are — how many connections you have and who they are, especially if you are in a sales environment or a position that requires customer interaction. Your level of connection and how you interact via LinkedIn speaks volumes about you as a contributing member of the workforce.

There are four distinct ways to connect with someone on LinkedIn. Each of these four connection opportunities allows you to begin a conversation with a LinkedIn member who can either be the person you need to speak with, or they can possibly give a referral to the right person at the company.

- Send an invitation to connect without a note.

- Send an invitation to connect with a short note — LinkedIn gives you the opportunity to write a note with the invitation (the number of characters is limited).

- Send an invitation to connect and a message using InMail if you are a Premium member of LinkedIn.

- Send a message without sending an invitation to connect. Although your message infers that you are seeking a new or different position, the message when requesting a connection should be to start a discussion about the company. Here are two examples:

  1. "Dear (first name), I would welcome an opportunity to speak with you about (company name). Please let me know a good day and time for us to have a conversation."

  2. "Dear (first name), I have researched your organization, and I am interested in learning more about your company. Please

let me know a good day and time for a conversation, and I will make myself available."

As you send out more connection requests you will see an increase in the daily number of LinkedIn notifications on your computer or smart phone. At the top of your LinkedIn profile, there is a navigation bar with several icons: Home, My Network, Jobs, Messaging, and Notifications. When you receive a notification, take time to review what is happening inside your network. The daily notifications are special milestones such as birthdays, promotions, job changes, new positions, or perhaps a new posting or article your connection took time to write or share. When you see notifications coming through, take a moment to comment with a thumbs-up, a like, or a congratulations message — all positive communication will enhance your networking.

In today's digital world your peers are looking for instant gratification; give it to them — it is all part of the networking climate. I do appreciate it when one of my connections comments or reacts to something I've posted! Your peers will reciprocate, and this is where relationships begin. These small gestures open the door to continued dialogue AND quite possibly a future opportunity.

Let's review the Jobs navigation icon at the top of your LinkedIn home page. Using artificial intelligence, LinkedIn scans the information in your profile and will notify or flag you when there is an opening at a specific company in a specific role that might be a fit. Plus, you can customize the settings to receive notifications for certain types of job openings.

If you click on the Jobs navigation icon and then select the My Jobs link, you can begin saving specific job descriptions for companies or positions that you may be interested in now or in the future. Let's take it a step further. In the My Jobs section, click on the blue link: Browse jobs for me (see Figure 3).

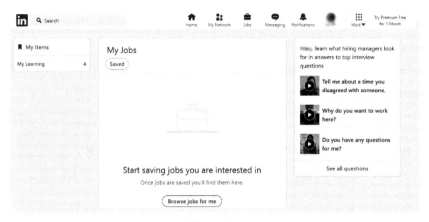

Figure 3.

You can now begin setting up your individualized company criteria along with positioning. LinkedIn allows you to search by title, skills, or company in addition to location (city, state, and ZIP Code). LinkedIn is user friendly, and it will walk you through each step to ensure optimum lead exposure and job-search criteria and notifications. This section will have suggested job searches based on your profile as seen in Figure 4.

As you scroll through this section, you will see suggested opportunities you may want to consider based on your profile and past search history. LinkedIn even shows you if the company is actively recruiting, how many applicants have submitted their resume, and if you have any potential connections at the company.

If a company catches your eye and you would like more information, hover your mouse over the company name and right-click on a Windows computer or control-click on a Mac. Now you can see the company details, for example: how many employees currently work at the company, job description, and in some cases the salary range, how many candidates have applied for the position, and how many company employees are on LinkedIn.

We strongly suggest you take time to set up the following areas: My Jobs, Job Alerts, Salary, and Skill Assessments (Figure 4). For additional features click on the More tab. LinkedIn also provides the most common interview questions, salary, resume builder, and more (Figure 5) as well as suggested jobs based on your profile and search history (Figures 6 and 7). Using these LinkedIn features coupled with the guidelines described in this chapter will enhance your job search.

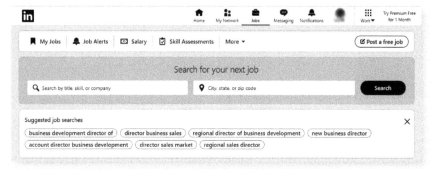

Figure 4.

Figure 5.

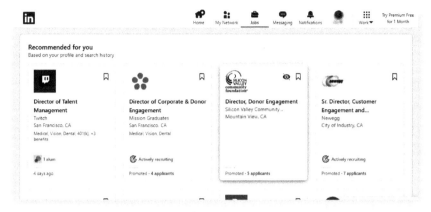

Figure 6.

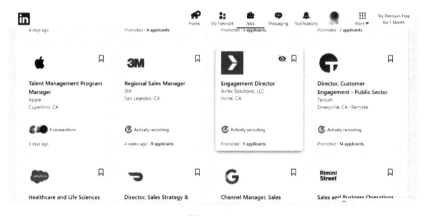

Figure 7.

The suggestions and screen captures presented in this book are just a few examples on how to best utilize LinkedIn as a job-search and networking tool. There is so much that this platform provides, and we cannot touch on all of its capabilities, but here is another area of importance: Go to your LinkedIn home page and click on your image on the left side of the page. This small action will open your profile page. Now look to the right where you will see

"People Also Viewed" (Figure 8). Scroll down the page, and you will notice "People You May Know" (Figure 9). This is another way to expand your network — by extending an invitation to connect.

You never know when a new connection may need a professional just like you. Timing is everything in the world of networking! Your new connection may have been recently promoted or may be leaving the organization and is charged with hiring his or her replacement. You may be just the solution one of these connections is looking for.

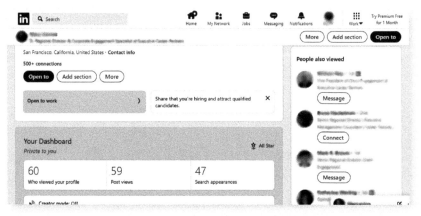

Figure 8.

Figure 9.

Jobs Created

Over the course of my coaching career, many jobs have been created for my clients — and, in a way, *by* my clients — using these networking skills. Reaching out and making a potential employer aware of your availability, interest, and knowledge is the key to finding the right position. Your conversation could begin with a mention of a recent press release regarding the company's growth or that person's recent promotion, or a company expansion under that manager's realm of responsibility. (You might consider asking if they are looking to replace that person's position.) Make specific references to their business and how you may be able to help impact their future growth. Soft skills is essential in this instance, as it will allow you to begin developing and nurturing relationships that will quite possibly lead to a future position.

The quickest way to build up your LinkedIn profile is to request references and endorsements. Ask a past colleague, supervisor, or subordinate to write about your time working together. It is perfectly OK to give your potential reference a few pointers on specifically what you are looking for their endorsement to say. For example, you can ask an employee who worked for you to provide a list of qualities you would like them to write about (for example, managerial style, training, mentoring, coaching, or how you helped the company achieve great success).

Once you receive the endorsement, LinkedIn gives you an opportunity to review the endorsement before posting, and you can request a change with perhaps a little guidance on your part. Most potential employers read endorsements to learn more about your work experiences.

In addition, you can set your profile to notify potential employers that you are seeking a new position. Access the Settings & Privacy section on your LinkedIn profile page by clicking on the Me navigation tab. You will see a drop-down menu that gives you access to your account and profile and walks you through several different settings pertaining to privacy including who can see your information. Here, you can set your profile to notify recruiters that you are open to new opportunities. Be careful, because if you are currently working and you turn on this feature you run the risk of your company's talent acquisition team stumbling across your information. However, for unemployed job seekers, this is an ideal way to notify recruiters and hiring influencers that you are looking for a new position.

Don't be afraid to explore. LinkedIn is very intuitive, and each tab and link will guide you to set up your account and provide information, so you can determine exactly how LinkedIn can use your data and what is seen (Figure 10).

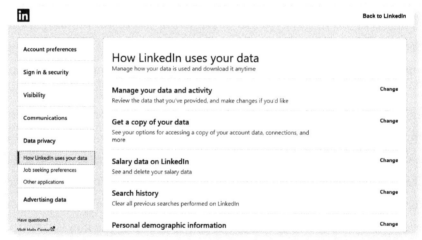

Figure 10.

Jobs Found

Now, I would like to apologize in advance if any human resource or recruiting professionals are part of our reading community — please take no offense to what I am about to say — but HR tends to be the gatekeeper and, quite frankly, seeks to control the hiring process. They are not revenue-producing entities, so they seek to be validated by making themselves needed, especially when it comes to the hiring process.

Most companies have a requisition process, meaning there is a hiring need that must go through the normal channels for approval. Once the requisition is approved, the recruiter or talent acquisition professional steps in. Typically, this recruitment professional holds a brief conversation with the hiring manager for clarification about the position, that is, their wants, needs, and so forth. They discuss the job description and ask as many questions as they can, but do they really know what that manager is looking for?

In my decades of experience working with recruiters and hiring managers, the job description usually does not outline the depth and breadth of a specific job description. On numerous occasions I have presented resumes to clients only to find out that the job description was incomplete, as the requirement only highlighted a small portion of the actual job. That is why we highly recommend you — the job seeker — take your job search into your own hands by "becoming your own recruiter." This means you are primarily responsible for finding your next position instead of relying on someone else to do this for you. You — and you alone — are the best person to land the right position with the right company. Remember, it's your career!

Start by making a list of the essential aspects of your ideal career opportunity. This will start you on the path to discovering what is most important to you, and it will help you further define your passions. What does your ideal job look like? Does it provide room for growth and advancement? What does advancement look like? Create a plan and path to get where you want to be in the next three, five, and ten years. Does this path give you an opportunity for mentoring or to be mentored?

Perhaps you enjoy and are skilled at managing a team or maybe you want to learn how to manage a budget, or you want more involvement in the profit-and-loss process. Are you open to relocation and if so where? Are you looking for a global *Fortune* 100/500 company, or does a smaller, more intimate environment appeal to you? And let us not forget about the thousands of start-ups that may be looking for someone just like you. Are you willing to take a leap of faith with a less stable but exciting start-up environment? When you answer these questions, you will have a clearer path to find the right career with the right company.

Now, if you can see the vision, start exploring companies that are of interest in the industry you have targeted. Begin making a list of companies that are of interest to you, so you can begin researching these companies to understand if they are a fit with your career goals. Most company websites highlight their leadership team on their websites. There is a lot to be uncovered with these website biographies. Seek out those hiring influencers and connect with them on LinkedIn.

If your job search is urgent, send a message to those hiring influencers with your resume and tell them how you can make an impact to their bottom line and future growth. Share how your accomplishments and professional skills can be a value to the company. Additionally, send them an email (email addresses can easily be found on the company's website or in a Google search). Let them know you would welcome a brief conversation or ask if they would be willing to introduce you to someone who can help you get connected for an immediate position or future consideration.

If your career or job search is not urgent, send a message to the influencer saying that you are interested in knowing more about the organization. As noted previously you can also mention the person's recent promotion or a company announcement as an ice breaker. Most high-level executives rarely receive letters with these types of messages or letters of engagement. Be bold! Take the steps that others are not willing to take or are too scared to do! This is an important key to your future success.

Let's take this to the next level. Let's say a vice president of engineering gets back to you and thanks you for your information but at this time he/she is not hiring. And the VP goes on to say that the company will keep your information on file. Be bold and ask if the VP knows of anyone in their professional network who may need someone with your education, knowledge, and professional skill set. Most of the time when I have requested a referral like this I have received a helpful response and a new connection.

Again, take actions that others are either too lazy or too scared to do, and you will get results. It's your career — it's your choice! Take the steps that very few others will. What do you have to lose? And let us come full circle for a moment, in our example, you should reach out to that VP of engineering every couple of months with your continued interest until you are given an opportunity to discuss a potential role in the organization.

Use all means possible to network as professionally and efficiently as possible. Do not rely on just one connection or one message to get your information into the right hands. Be strategic, be bold, and take the steps that others are not willing to do. If you practice just a couple of the suggested steps in this chapter, you will see more activity, conversations, and potentially your next offer with a great company that aligns with your future growth and objectives.

CHAPTER 6

Employment Agencies, Staffing Companies, and Recruiters

IN YOUR JOB SEARCH YOU MAY ASK FOR HELP from a staffing company or an employment agency. Although we have detailed the necessary steps for you to "become your own recruiter," you may want to use these services to help you find the right position.

The history of employment agencies and staffing companies is quite interesting. For centuries companies have depended upon the services of outside agencies to support their human resource requirements. Companies from virtually every industry have outsourced their recruiting for every conceivable open position for centuries. Here are some interesting facts about employment agencies and staffing companies (Source: https://www.bighrc. com › blog › history-of-recruitment):

- The world's first recruitment agency was started by Henry Robinson in 1653.

- The first known private employment agency was Gabbitas and Thring, founded in 1873 by John Gabbitas to recruit schoolmasters for public schools in England.

- Fred Winslow founded the first U.S. employment agency in 1893 as an engineering agency.

- In the U.S., there are about 20,000 staffing and recruiting firms, which operate over 39,000 offices.

- Temporary and staffing agencies in the U.S. account for over $170 billion in revenue.

- Staffing and recruitment agencies are regulated by the Employment Agencies Act of 1973.

- Since the 1940s the staffing industry has grown twice as fast as the economy. (Source: American Staffing Association).

- Employment and staffing agencies serve almost every industry:
  - 37 percent — Industrial labor
  - 28 percent — Office: clerical and administrative
  - 13 percent — Managerial
  - 13 percent — Engineering, information technology, scientific
  - 9 percent — Healthcare

Executive Search and Employment Agencies

Full-time employment agencies help companies recruit talent for their open positions. They function as a supplement to a company's human resources department. As demand grows for hiring, so does recruiting. The employment agency charges a fee for a placement that, in most cases, will cost the company less than using the human resources department's in-house recruiting staff. The employment agency offers specific recruiting expertise and works with a client company, creating a win/win for both organizations.

Some general employment agencies will recruit and place applicants with virtually every skill set. Some employment agencies specifically concentrate in one industry such as engineering, information technology, or healthcare, or they focus on a certain level of leadership such as C-level executives (for example, CEO, CFO, CIO).

Employment agencies — whether you call them agencies, headhunters, or executive search firms — have virtually the same goal: recruiting, screening, and presenting a candidate for consideration for an open position. The model for a majority of these agencies is called *contingency search*. They work with a company with no up-front fees and are paid only when a candidate is successfully placed.

A retained search is when an agency contracts with a company to place a candidate in a mid- to high-level position. The company pays part of the agency's fee at the beginning of the search and the final payment once the candidate is placed. In some cases a retained search agency will receive an initial fee, an additional payment after thirty or sixty days. and the final payment once the candidate is placed.

Interestingly, years ago I contacted a company that I wanted to work for that had already contracted with a retained executive search firm. After I negotiated directly with the company for over three months I was offered the position I wanted. Even though I did not work through the executive search firm the company was required to pay them a fee.

Staffing Companies

The temporary services industry began in earnest during World War II. With so many soldiers leaving for military duty there were many open positions that created a need for the modern-era staffing agency. The industry continued to grow over the next two decades. (Do you remember the Kelly Girl ads in the late 1960s?)

The temporary staffing industry has continued to grow over the past six decades, and its growth parallels some of the advances in technology. For an industry that began as a "necessary evil" it has evolved into a professional and integral part of our workforce. Although at the beginning of the COVID-19 pandemic the temporary staffing industry experienced a downturn in business, it quickly rebounded to pre-pandemic levels. In fact, due to the need for a remote and flexible workforce, the temporary services industry is seeing massive growth in the use of temporary labor.

Temporary staffing firms help companies find qualified talent to support specific projects until the project is completed. Companies will contract to staffing firms and employment agencies to supplement their human resources department. The company and the staffing company will agree on a set hourly rate that will be paid to the temporary worker. The staffing agency will then bill the company a rate that will include the worker's pay rate plus the staffing company's direct and indirect costs in addition to a margin for profit. Large companies in industries such as aerospace, banking, finance, and healthcare spend hundreds of millions of dollars every year for the services of temporary and consulting workers.

Since the early 1960s companies have also used staffing agencies to replace their probationary periods for new employees. The past fifty years have seen new state and federal guidelines and laws concerning employment hiring and terminations. Most organizations have a probationary period for new employees that can range from one month to four months. As these guidelines and laws have evolved over the past five decades they have made the termination of a new employee difficult at best.

In order to comply with local, state, and federal employment laws — while maintaining as much flexibility as possible — many organizations have reached out to temporary staffing companies and created a manner in which they can hire a new employee for a short period of time (thirty, sixty, or ninety days or more) to see if the employee is both a technical and cultural fit. This is called *temp to hire*. By contracting to a staffing company for a temp to hire engagement, the temporary worker or contractor is not an employee of the company but of the agency. The company, after an agreed period of time, can offer the person a full-time position or terminate the temp's employment without documentation or reason. In these cases, the staffing organization is responsible for the "end of assignment" paperwork.

Using a third-party recruiter or agency can be a great experience if you control the manner in which your information is given to a potential employer. Too many job seekers let these support services dictate the manner in which they look for a job. Agencies and their recruiters are most usually working for a for-profit organization and, therefore, their only goal is to place a candidate in an open position — even sometimes if the candidate is only remotely qualified.

I have spent the majority of my working career in the staffing industry as a recruiter, manager, executive, and business owner. In over four decades, I have seen vast changes as the recruiting process has matured. Early on as a "green" recruiter I was told to present as many applicants as possible in the hopes that someone would get hired. We were instructed not to waste our time calling back candidates who were rejected for a position, since our time was valuable, and we needed to begin working on the next open position. We were focused on the number of people we could hire — it was quantity versus quality. Before the 1980s it was almost unheard of to match a candidate on both behavioral and technical qualifications. Times have changed!

Over the past forty years there has been a dramatic cultural shift in the American job market. Remaining with a company for your entire career is no longer the norm. The growing number of temporary and contract work opportunities is here to stay. Some staffing experts suggest that over 40 percent of the workforce will consist of temporary and contract workers by 2025. Yet the future of the temporary staffing industry depends on the economy. For example, when the unemployment rate is low companies will turn to staffing organizations. A low unemployment rate means the applicant pool is limited, there is a lack of qualified applicants, and competition from other employers is high. When the unemployment rate is high there is an increase in the number of qualified applicants available for open positions. The staffing industry usually sees a downturn in business during these times. Yet even though the staffing industry directly responds to the economy's volatility, it remains a large part of the employment marketplace.

Agency Recruiters

Recruiters from entry level to the most senior recruiter are reaching out to prospective candidates to fill their open positions. Some of the best executive search organizations employ recruiters who are experienced and understand the art of recruiting. They will interview you, question you, and determine your qualifications for the position.

But should you use a recruiter? There are many reasons to use a recruiter but just as many reasons not to use a recruiter.

Once you have mastered the Art of Networking you can "become your own recruiter." Every step I have outlined in the networking chapter represents the same tasks that a recruiter performs. In some cases you are doing more than the average recruiter by making your job search personal. I am confident that by employing the techniques in the networking chapter you can find the position and career you are looking for without having a recruiter work as your agent. Remember that using a recruiter to help you find the right position with the right company takes networking out of the equation. In most cases recruiters and agencies prohibit you from contacting their client company, and you have no vehicle to gain an understanding of the company or the company's management.

A recruiter's job is not to find you a job. Recruiters are hired by businesses that are looking for employees to fill their open positions. Staffing and employment agency recruiters usually work on a low salary and a commission or just a commission. In many cases you are competing with other candidates who have the same or similar background as you, and the decision to interview and subsequently hire you is out of your control. Recruiters may send many resumes for one open position in the hopes that one of their candidates will be considered. (It's like throwing a box of resumes against the wall and hoping one of them sticks!) Companies are inundated with stacks of resumes, and the review period can take a long time.

As mentioned earlier, some companies use ATS systems to screen all resumes including those submitted by recruiting companies. If your resume does not have the keywords in the job description you may be disqualified immediately. In some cases staffing companies will submit ten or more resumes for one opening hoping that one of their candidates will be accepted for an interview. When I owned a staffing company, in an effort to stand out from our competition, we would let our clients (the hiring companies) know that we would send no more than three qualified resumes for each opening. This helped to ensure our client would not be reviewing resumes that were not qualified for the open position. By doing this the client was well aware that each candidate was fully vetted and qualified for the opportunity. Today many staffing organizations are following my model in order to decrease the number of unqualified applicants submitted for consideration.

Using a recruiter from an agency or a staffing company can be both a positive and a negative. The benefit comes from having an additional resource to help you find the position you want. If you are looking for a temporary or consulting position, using a third-party representative can satisfy your immediate needs. As I mentioned, staffing companies may have a temp-to-hire position with a company that you have chosen, and the position is perfect for you. In this case using an outside agency is the vehicle you need to settle into your career.

The not-so-positive result of using a recruiter to help you find a position is simply that this person is not dedicated to your career. As I discussed, a recruiter is not interested in finding you a position but, instead, is working to place as many applicants as possible to support their client companies. Yet there is a way you can work with a recruiter and have them support your goal of finding the position you want.

- Ask the recruiter to send you a copy of your resume that they sent to their client.
  - In some cases a recruiting company will alter or change your resume, so it appears that you have the necessary qualification for the position. You want to make sure the qualifications that are presented to their client are factual and correct.
  - The recruiting company may present your resume without your contact information, so their client cannot contact you directly. This is standard practice with both staffing and employment agencies.

- Ask the recruiter about the client and their business relationship and ask them to update you through every step of the process, for example:
  - When was your resume presented to their client? You want to make sure the recruiter knows that time is of the essence for you.

  - How long before you will receive feedback on your resume? Recruiters usually know the length of time it takes for their client to respond to their resume submittals. Also, ask that they let you know if you have not been accepted to move to the next step in the hiring process. Most agencies will not call to let you know that you are no longer being considered — they will wait for you to call them!

  - How many positions or similar positions are open with their client? Some clients have multiple openings, which can open up additional opportunities for you.

  - How many candidates are they submitting for consideration for this position? This will give you an idea as to whether they are just "dumping" your resume on the client. If they inform you that they have submitted ten candidates for one opening — well, I would be skeptical of any positive outcome. If however they are submitting only one or two candidates for the position it could possibly be a great opportunity for you.

- Are they competing with other agencies? Some of their business clients will contract with several agencies, so their jobs can be filled. If several agencies are involved, your chances of securing this position have just diminished. If they have an exclusive agreement with this client your chances of success are substantially increased.

- How long has the recruiter been working with this business client? If the recruiter or the agency has been working with the client for a long period of time you can assume they have a good working relationship with the client and your chances of success are increased. If they inform you that this is a new client you may be a "test" resume for their company to secure that company as a new client. In other words, you need to let the recruiter know that you understand the process, so that your time is spent wisely.

- Remember this whole process is about you! The recruiter is working for a recruitment company that is supporting a specific business client — don't let yourself become part of their "business as usual" process. By asking the recruiter pointed questions and asking for timely feedback, you are letting the recruiter know that they are also working for you.

Corporate Recruiters in the HR Department

Recruiting has always been part of a company's personnel department, which today may be called human resources, people development, department of people, or talent acquisition. A personnel or human resources department is the support area that companies depend on to manage the day-to-day issues regarding the employees of the company. Human resources has evolved dramatically over the past thirty years. We now find so many divisions, subdivisions, and departments that it is nearly unrecognizable when compared to the personnel departments of the past.

In larger companies you will find that the human resources department includes recruiting, employee relations, diversity, change management, instructional design, benefits, wage and salary analysis, job analysis, job descriptions, training, risk management, and more. You get the picture! Human resources is not only concerned with recruiting. It is a full-on department that manages the employee experience.

To recruit new employees, mid-size and large organizations often have several levels of in-house corporate recruiters. Some large corporations have employees who are initial screeners (they screen resumes that have successfully made it through the ATS process) and decide which applicants will be forwarded to the next level of screening for a possible interview. In most cases, this is the point where many job seekers receive the standard letter saying they are not qualified for the position or that the position has been filled by a more qualified or internal candidate.

The next level of review includes more senior in-house recruiters who will read and analyze your resume for an initial screening call or email. Other recruiters will conduct the initial interview by phone or video call. In a few of the larger companies these senior recruiters will conduct a series of interviews to screen out the least qualified or behaviorally unfit candidates. In a few instances the recruiter who is interviewing you may have little or no understanding of the position for which they are recruiting. If the position is technical you may be screened by a recruiter who is just reading a job description. In fact, the lack of technical knowledge applies to most positions. A recruiter interviewing a salesperson who has no sales experience can easily disqualify even the most qualified candidate.

Granted, the recruiting department for companies is a necessity. If you have presented your resume to an organization through a website or an online job board you will be considered first by the human resources' recruiting department. Your resume will be screened and evaluated by someone who may not understand the depth of your background and who may not fully understand the position's requirements. Does your resume tell them everything they need to know for you to be considered for the position? Of course not! This perhaps is the greatest argument for networking! Connecting with a manager in the specific department in which you want to work can be the best and most efficient way to interact with the company's recruiting department — this is a networking referral.

If the company you have selected has a human resources department that controls all the initial stages of the hiring process, having a conversation with a company's hiring manager will be your first step in meeting the HR department's recruiter. For example, if you connected with a company manager who has told you that you must first speak with or communicate with human resources, you can ask the name of the person in human resources with whom you need to speak. You can then reach out to this HR person with a referral from the manager. Simply put, a cold call to the recruiting department will, in most cases, result in them asking you to submit your resume through the website or a job board. Remember the "black hole" of lost or forgotten resumes? Yet if you were to reach out to human resources saying you were referred to them by a company manager, you could possibly begin the resume submittal process with a conversation and potentially get a foot in the door.

If, however, the company's recruiting department is a "rubber stamp" then reaching out to them is just adding another unnecessary step to the hiring process. In this case the managers of each department control the hiring process. They will screen, select, and interview the candidates they feel are qualified for the position. Once they have selected a candidate they will refer that person to human resources for the onboarding process. Again, this is another argument for researching, connecting, and networking with the individuals who are responsible for hiring.

Most corporate recruiters work on multiple openings. So your resume and your name will not be familiar to them unless you have personally reached out to them. Gaining an introduction to the recruiter can, in many cases, ensure you are one of the first to be considered for a position. You are not just a resume — you are a person with a name!

Corporate recruiters can delay, enhance, or derail the hiring process. When the hiring process is delayed it is because employment is not a priority! That is not to say that companies don't have a sense of urgency to hire additional or replacement staff. Simply, recruiters have other responsibilities and, in some cases, identifying, screening, and interviewing candidates is not first on their list. They can enhance the hiring process by expediting the interview and referral process to the next level in the hiring chain. And finally, they can derail the process by not identifying the most qualified candidate — YOU!

Suffice to say corporate recruiters are an important part of the hiring process, and it is incumbent upon you to use this department to your benefit. Directly contacting human resources because you are aware of a position that both fits your skill set and your interest will most likely ensure your resume falls into the proverbial "black hole." But your networking will pay off when you are introduced to the human resources person who is handling your resume. You are not just another applicant trying to get a position — you have now been referred to the person who will review your qualifications. You will need to successfully pass through the human resources screening process to secure the position you want. Once you are introduced to the company's corporate recruiters, work to gain their trust, so they can assist in expediting the hiring process.

Employment agencies, staffing companies, and corporate recruiters within the IIR department all play an important role in the hiring process.

They can be the key to getting the position you want. Keep in mind, though, that employment agencies and staffing companies are interested in placing you at their client companies — for the most part they are not interested in your career goals. As we discussed earlier, by following the networking plan outlined in Chapter 5 you can be your best recruiter! If, however, you are looking for a consulting or temporary position, it can be helpful to use a staffing company to satisfy your interim needs.

CHAPTER 7

Your Interview

YES, THE DREADED INTERVIEW. The component of the hiring process that will either have you on the road to the next step in your career or seeking out another company. The interview process does not have to be as stressful as you may think. I will show you in the following pages how to make the interview YOUR INTERVIEW — and not the company's interview of you.

In my many years of preparing candidates for interviews I have seen some who are comfortable, some who are hesitant, and some who dread even the thought of participating in an interview. If you are comfortable with the interview process, you will find interview tips in this chapter that will make your interview experience easier. If you are hesitant or dreading this part of the hiring process, I am sure your level of comfort will be elevated, so you will enjoy the interview once you understand the unique methods of how to make the interview YOUR interview.

The interview is one of the final steps in securing a new position. There are two critical ideas to consider prior to the interview to make sure you get the results you want.

First, the result is not always "getting the job." Of course you are participating in the interview process, because you are interested in the position. Yet in some instances, you may find during the interview that you are no longer interested in working for this company. The interviewers could mention some issues about the company, or they may let you know about the work environment, which is not in line with your goals. There are numerous comments or visual cues you may experience during the interview that could change your mind about moving to the next steps with this company. Sometimes you will be surprised by a negative comment from the interviewer that may change your mind about the position. For example, you may be told that there is excessive overtime or that the company is being sold and the interviewer is not sure what the future holds for both the company and the employees.

Second and perhaps most importantly, your interview truly is YOUR INTERVIEW! A company may have a requirement to fill a position, and that requirement will be filled by a qualified candidate — this may or may not be you. Your qualifications and experience are the reason you have been asked to interview for the position. You have every right to accept or reject an offer of employment. As you learn more about the company, its culture, and the work environment you can decide if this position is right for you.

Of course, the interview process is a two-way street. But if you understand that you are also interviewing the interviewer and the company, you can be assured that you will achieve a comfort level during the interview that will allow you to discuss your qualifications in the most positive manner. In most cases the company will fill the position with the person they believe is most qualified, and the information you share during your interview can help ensure they choose you. If you want to begin or further your career with this position, then you can take the next step to onboarding, negotiating your compensation package, and selecting a start date.

But if it is not the right position for you don't hesitate to walk away from the interview. Of course, you don't get up and abruptly leave the room or Zoom meeting, but you can gracefully end the interview by letting the company know that you don't want to waste their time or yours, because you feel this is not the right company or position for you. Remember, this is just one position with one company. You will interview with other companies and for other positions that will be more synergistic with your needs and wants in a position.

I cannot tell you how many times I have seen clients participate in an interview and subsequently take a position they knew was not right for them. And the results were mostly the same. Within a short period of time they were once again looking for a new position.

Keep in mind the advice in our networking chapter. You are just looking for one job or one contact who will allow you to connect with the right person at a company you have selected. If the position is not right for you, don't take it just because it is offered! Since you were able to secure this interview because of your background and networking skills, you need to be confident that you will get another interview with a company you want to work for — one that is more compatible with your career goals.

The reason so many people are nervous before and during the interview is that they feel if they don't get this particular job, they will never find another one. Or perhaps they are just uncomfortable speaking with people they do not know. It is always difficult to speak with someone for the first time when that person has perceived control of the meeting.

If you are desperate for a job due to family and financial circumstances, then by all means take the position knowing it is a temporary fix for you. However, if you are seeking a long-term career position, you can be confident that there will be other companies and multiple offers. Remember, it is YOUR interview and YOUR choice as to whether you accept an offer. Once you realize you are in control of the interview most of the angst over interviewing will disappear.

Of course, you might be nervous in anticipation of and during the interview. Regardless of your ability to communicate during an interview, it's human nature to ask, "Am I doing OK?" Even after the interview, you might second-guess yourself. How many times have you completed a meeting or a conversation and said to yourself, "I wish I had said …" or "I should have let them know that I am …"? By understanding that you are also interviewing the interviewer, you can decrease your level of discomfort.

I have given hundreds of workshops and presentations over the past thirty years. I have observed my audience and realize that most people only spend a limited amount of time listening. I heard someone say once that you spend 80 percent of your time not listening to the presenter. In fact, I use this 80 percent rule to start my presentation by asking my participants to give me just another 10 percent with the guarantee that they will leave the presentation or workshop learning the subject matter of the presentation.

This is the same case with an interview. Both you and the interviewer will not hear or listen to everything that is said. It is important, therefore, that during the interview you focus on the questions and respond with your prepared answers. It is just as important not to second-guess yourself during the interview. Stay focused and on subject, and I can assure you that your interview will be successful. Success, however, is not about getting the job. It could mean you have discovered that this company or environment does not fit your career goals. It is then time to graciously end the interview.

Prior to your interview you should prepare for everything you can control. Never forget that this is YOUR interview. Even if this is your dream job, you have every right to ask questions prior to and during the interview process. Develop a plan for your interview that includes the following action steps:

- *Be prepared for the unexpected as you begin your interview* — By following this plan you can control everything in the interview that you can anticipate. Of course, there will be subjects and questions you will not expect. But preparing yourself for what you can control will make it much easier to cope with those subjects that arise that you did not expect.

- *Research the company* — Review the website to learn who is on the management team, how long the company has been in business, and so forth. Also, look at the reviews (both good and bad). A quick search of Google reviews, Glassdoor, and the Better Business Bureau can give you information about a company that can make you even more comfortable during the interview process.

- A former client interviewed for a sales management position with a local company. He did not research the company prior to the interview. Yet he aced the interview and was offered the job. After he returned home he researched the company only to find that there were over thirty poor reviews from previous employees. He was interested in the position but asked me what he should do. I suggested that prior to accepting the position he request a meeting with the president of the company to ask him about all the negative reviews. He met with the president and was told that all thirty reviews were from "disgruntled" employees. My client continued to probe him about the reviews and received only excuses and non-answers. In the end, the second meeting made him uncomfortable about accepting the offer. He declined the position and was able to find another position within weeks. This is a perfect example of knowing that if you don't take this job there will be another one on the horizon.

- *Review the LinkedIn profiles* — Look at the profiles of the management team and all interviewers:

  - How much experience do they have?

  - Review their references on LinkedIn.

  - How long have they been with the company? If the interviewers have been with the company for over three years, you can be assured they will be able to offer insight on the company including its culture and operations. If, however, they have recently accepted a position with the company, they may not be able to give you the information you need. Knowing how long they have been employed by the company will give you some insight on how to conduct your interview.

- Do you have any mutual contacts on LinkedIn? Reach out to your mutual contacts to get a better understanding of the interviewers — some of their interests, goals, and how much they are involved with the company.

- Get to know as much as you can about their background and experience. Researching the interviewers can give you a comfort level, so you can have a successful interview.

- *Ask the person setting up the interview about the company's dress code* — Always dress "one step up" from the company's standard dress code. In today's relaxed work environment it is important to respect the interview process. So if a company's employees dress in shorts and flip-flops you should dress in acceptable business casual attire (not shorts and flip-flops). Now if a company lets you know that the attire is formal (for example, suit and tie or dress or skirt), it would not be advisable to dress one step up — tuxedos and formal dresses are not necessary! You can always adjust what you are wearing after you arrive for the interview. For example, if you are dressed in a jacket or a buttoned sweater, you can always take off the jacket or sweater and place it on your lap. Be careful not to over-dress as this could make the interviewer uncomfortable.

- A few years ago I gave a presentation to a group of Veterans discussing the secrets of navigating the hiring process. I arrived in a suit and tie only to find that everyone in attendance was dressed very casually. I immediately took off my jacket and tie and mentioned that "I guess I was overdressed." My comment made everyone comfortable for the remainder of the presentation. So by observing something as simple as being overdressed, you can set the right tone for the interview.

- ***Develop a list of ten questions you want to ask about the company, the company culture, and the management style*** — Note that none of these questions should be about salary, benefits, or time off. Also, make sure you are attentive during the interview, because some of your questions may be answered before you get a chance to ask them. One of the biggest mistakes in an interview is to not listen and then ask a question that has already been answered! Here are a few sample interview questions to ask:

  - "Can you tell me about the company culture and your mission for your employees?" — The response you are looking for is a discussion about how the company treats its employees. Are the employees treated as "workers" or are they treated as partners? The culture of a company can determine your level of comfort during the work week. If you are not comfortable with the environment, you could become less productive. It has been my experience that this question can reveal so much about a company. Many people love to talk about their work and themselves. In a few cases the answers you receive could help you decide whether or not to take the position.

- "What is it like to work here?" — This question is similar to the question on company culture but takes your inquiry to the next level. You will most probably receive answers that run the spectrum of responses. Those employees who enjoy their jobs will most probably respond with positive accolades about the company, the management, and the people. Those who may possibly be considering leaving the company or are not happy with their position may give you information that is not as positive as those who are enjoying their positions. Keep in mind that the information you receive will be an opinion — but an opinion that can give you valuable information about the company and the management team's relationship with employees.

- "How many people work in this department?" — Knowing the size of the department gives you an idea of the workload and the number of people managed.

- "What is the percentage of turnover in the department?" — This is an important question. This is a touchy question for some interviewers, so be sure you are comfortable asking about the attrition rate in the department. On the one hand, if the turnover in a department is low you can be assured it is a good place to work. If, however, the turnover is high you can assume the work environment or the management style may be an issue. In some instances a high attrition rate may not be due to the company or management but the industry. In the staffing industry, for example, the turnover for first-year recruiters is over 30 percent. In this case it is not the management or the work environment but the true nature of the position.

- "What is the management style?" — There are many different and unique management styles. Thankfully, many old styles of management have become obsolete. Management by intimidation and fear have become management styles of the past. And you may have found that micro-managers can prohibit your productivity. You want to find a management style that makes you comfortable. If you work best with a hands-on manager then this may be the job for you. On the other hand, if you enjoy the freedom of working independently you may want to find a management style that empowers workers to be creative with limited supervision.

- "How long has this position been open?" — If the position has been open for more than two months you can ask why they have not hired anyone. The stock answer will be, "We are looking for the right candidate." You can follow that response by asking about the top five requirements they are looking for in a candidate. This response could be both technical and behavioral. For example, they may be seeking a candidate with a specific background (e.g., a unique platform or software program), or they may let you know that one of the most important characteristics is your ability to be an essential part of the company culture. It has been my experience that many companies have created job descriptions that are virtually unfillable! That is, the company has written a job description with a lengthy set of requirements that simply doesn't exist. You will find these "unfillable" positions during a job market where there is an abundance of candidates and very few jobs. In this case, the company has the luxury of hiring a candidate that meets nearly all requirements. In the reverse market (more jobs are available than qualified candidates), a company that has ten requirements for a position may offer you the position if you only meet seven of the requirements. As noted earlier, carefully read the job description to understand the position requirements.

- "How soon do you want to make a hire?" — You will get two answers to this question: "As soon as we find the right candidate" or "We expect to fill this position as soon as possible." If the former statement is the response, this is your opportunity to make the case for yourself as the most qualified candidate for the position. In the second answer, you now have a chance to expedite the process by shining during the interview. If you are told they are looking for the right candidate you can ask a follow-up question such as, "What does the perfect candidate look like?" The answer to this question could open up additional dialogue and provide insight into the company, the position, and whether or not you want to pursue this job.

- "How many candidates are you interviewing? Are any of these internal candidates?" — The answers will give you additional insight into the company's hiring process. If they are interviewing only three or four candidates, they may have done sufficient screening of the resumes that were submitted. If, however, you are told they are interviewing ten or more candidates, the company may be searching for the "perfect" candidate that does not exist. If you are comfortable during the interview and you have established a rapport with the interviewer, it is OK to ask — in a very tactful manner — "Where do I stand as compared to the others you have interviewed?" If you ask this question and you are told they are interviewing five candidates and you are the fourth interview and are number four on their list, you can assume you will not get the job! If, however, you are told that you are the leading candidate or the number-two candidate, your chances of securing the position are high. This question allows you to be comfortable at the end of the interview. No guessing about what the interviewers thought of you.

- "Is this a new or a replacement position?" — If this is a new position you can ask why this additional position has been created. (Be careful with this question as it may have been addressed in a previous response when the interviewer spoke of the company's growth.) If it is a replacement, you can also ask why the last person left the position. Were they promoted? Did they leave for a better position? Were they unhappy with their position? You will not always get an answer to this question, but it shows your level of interest in the company and the position.

- "What are your expectations during the first thirty, sixty, and ninety days?" — Obviously it takes time to adjust to your new environment. The reason for this question is to find out how their expectations align with your abilities and the time you may think you need to adapt to your new job. Some organizations may be more lenient, allowing you time to adjust, while others may expect you to "hit the ground running." By understanding what is expected during the first months on the job you will virtually eliminate the possibility of any surprises.

- *Prior to the interview ask how many company employees will be involved in the interview* — It is YOUR interview, and you need to have as much information as you can prior to the interview. Always prepare for the unexpected.

- So many interviews end in rejection, because the interviewee did not ask the person who set up the interview for the number of people involved in the interview. You arrive for the interview thinking you will be speaking to one person and — surprise! — you are being interviewed by a group of three or four company employees. You had expected to speak to one person and were prepared for the interview. Now you are facing two or three additional interviewers — all in a group — and your comfort level has disappeared.

- Additionally, if you don't ask about the number of people involved in the interview process, you could be informed upon arrival that you will be interviewing with three or four employees in a series of individual interviews. You were not prepared for this situation or the amount of time it will involve, and you have lost your level of comfort.

- Asking questions will allow you to control your part of the interview. There are enough surprises in life — don't let the format of your interview be a surprise!

Another way to lessen your discomfort during an in-person or video interview is to be aware of the surroundings. Let's say that you have just arrived for your interview and are taken into the office of the interviewer, or the video has just begun. Look around, see what they have in their office. Are there pictures of their family, sports trophies, posters, or other pictures that offer insight into some of their interests? In many cases, observing how the office is set up lets you develop talking points that will set both you and the interviewer at ease.

Most of the time observing the layout of the interviewer's office will set the tone for the interview. By observing the office surroundings you can develop additional talking points about their family (try not to get too personal), hobbies, and interests. From my experience, I have found that observing the office surroundings and commenting about them can make your interview experience more relaxed and enjoyable.

One of my clients interviewed with an entertainment company and noticed that the interviewer had a poster on his wall of his favorite movie. He immediately mentioned that he loved the movie, and this set a positive tone throughout the interview. He was offered the job and, interestingly, he and the manager have become close friends. This is just one example that being aware of your surroundings can lead to a successful interview.

Yet in some cases being observant can cause you to question whether or not you may want the position. Years ago I was interviewing for an executive position with a mid-size staffing company. I was waiting in the lobby, and the receptionist was in the lobby with a tape measure. She was making sure that the chairs in the reception area were all six inches apart and six inches from the wall. This seemed quite strange to me and made me uncomfortable. I wondered if a focus on unnecessary details or an odd perfectionism permeated the work environment.

After waiting for about ten minutes I was escorted to the office of the CEO. We had a few minutes of introductory talk before we began discussing the position. The first question I asked was about the receptionist and the tape measure — was this his idea or hers? He told me that it must have been the receptionist's idea, and that he would never do that. I took the position only to find out that measuring the chairs was the CEO's idea — and it was just one example of his controlling attitude. Suffice to say, my tenure with this company was not very long! Had he told me the truth, I am sure I would have ended the interview and continued looking for a position. Wherever possible, you want to control the interview process to make yourself comfortable. Getting an untruthful answer is a part of the interview process you cannot control. I had to rely on my instincts to make an informed decision. I was wrong!

I have always noted that the worst thing that can happen when you enter someone's office for an interview is that their desk is clear of any papers and there are no pictures or knickknacks that can give you the slightest information about the person who is interviewing you. Or you have been taken to a conference room for the interview where there is not a single clue about the company or the interviewers. If this is the case, you need to rely on your questions and your research. Extensive research before the interview is your key to a successful interview.

Be prepared for your interview and use every means possible to ensure you have a relaxed and enjoyable interview. I had a client with the most amazing story. She was a dentist who joined the U.S. Navy and spent over five years on active duty. Once she was separated from the Navy, she realized she did not want to be a dentist anymore. She enrolled in graduate school and received an MBA in finance. She had a great background, we wrote an attractive resume, and she was ready to start applying for positions as a financial analyst. She networked for hours over the next two weeks. Within a month she had three interviews at companies she had selected. Three interviews and not one job offer.

After each interview we discussed how she felt about the interview, and each time she told me she did not do well. She was extremely nervous, sweating, and felt she did not answer the questions in a coherent way. To say the least she was frustrated. We then spent over three hours discussing what she was nervous about. Together, we concluded that in each interview she felt she had limited options, and this *one* job was the only job available to her. After discussing the reason why she was feeling so much angst, she became convinced that each job opportunity was different, and there were an abundance of positions in her field.

Two weeks later she interviewed with a company she had selected and was offered a position. I spoke to her after the interview and, for the first time, she felt confident that she had done well in the interview. She not only did well, but she was offered the position at a salary higher than she had originally asked, and they wanted her to start almost immediately. That was six years ago, and she is still working at the same company today.

As a staffing executive, I was recruited by a major staffing firm to become a vice president of one of their large regional areas. They flew me to their corporate headquarters, and I was scheduled to interview with seven (count them, seven) vice presidents and senior executives in one day. After the fourth interview and just before a lunch interview with the executive vice president, I asked to be taken back to human resources. I knew I was not a good fit for this company, and the company was not a good fit for me. I informed the human resources manager that I was not interested in completing the interview process, and I was taking the next flight home. They, I am sure, were not happy with my decision, but it was the right decision for me. The reason I tell this story is to remind you that it is OK to say no to a potential employer — even in the midst of the interview process. If the position is not right for you or you are uncomfortable with the people and the surroundings, don't waste their time or yours. There is always another position for you to consider.

There is one other story that needs to be told. I interviewed a candidate for a recruiter position. Her background and experience were a perfect match for the position. She was experienced, well-spoken, and brought a "book of business" from her previous employer. There is an expression that you should never sell beyond the close — simply say just enough to get the job you want. After over an hour interviewing, I realized this candidate was rambling and talking about unrelated subjects. I guess you could say, "I had simply asked what time it was, and she told me how to build a clock!" Remember, say just enough to answer each question but not too much. You do not want to disqualify yourself from the position. I did not hire this recruiter.

The last thirty years has seen a dramatic change in the interviewing and hiring process. Significant changes began during the 1990s and have matured over the past three decades. In the world in which I grew up, employers were most interested in your ability to perform in the position. If you had a technical background, the key concern was how much technical knowledge you had about the product. If you had a sales background, the employer wanted to know how you would succeed in the sales position. I remember the first job I was offered as a recruiter. The regional manager did not care what kind of a person I was or if I would get along with the rest of the staff. During the interview, he was just interested in my background as an encyclopedia salesperson while I was attending college, because this proved I had the necessary communication skills for the position.

Today, hiring managers consider the person's soft skills along with his or her technical qualifications. Companies are not only looking for your ability to do the job but are also interested in how well you will fit into the culture of the company. In years past, your ability to perform in the position was perhaps 80 percent of the employer's decision to hire you. There was virtually very little behavioral consideration if you were qualified for the job. Of course, showing up to an interview with a negative attitude or dressed as if you were going the beach (unless you were applying for a lifeguard position) might result in a negative outcome.

The process of hiring will be in a constant state of change. Your ability to secure a position depends on your experience and background as well as how the interviewers perceive you will fit in with the company. Twenty years ago it would be safe to say that a successful interview consisted of 80 percent of your ability to perform in the position and 20 percent of how you may fit into the company. Further, in the past you may have had a single interview before receiving an offer for the position. Today, many companies will conduct three, four, and even five interviews before they decide to offer the position to the selected candidate.

Remember the company with the receptionist measuring the chairs in the lobby? During my interview process, this company had me interview with all the division managers (even though they would be reporting to me), so they could give their input to the CEO before he made a final decision. I found out later that three out of the four managers wanted me to join the company. Yes, I was offered the position, but I have seen in many instances that one less-than-positive recommendation from an interviewer can get you rejected from a position.

In one situation, a client interviewed with a major software firm. She was asked to interview with five different managers during a two-week period. The first four managers gave her glowing recommendations and the fifth, for some unknown reason, did not feel she was right for the company. She did not get the job! When I debriefed her about the interview, I found out that she did not review each of the interviewer's profiles on LinkedIn. Had she done so perhaps the outcome would have been different. These situations of multiple interviews coupled with an interview process that equally divides experience and behavior makes the process of preparing for an interview so much more important. Prepare and overprepare for your interview, as you will need to expect the unexpected!

Types of Interviews

There are three types of interviews: the formal, informal, and unprepared interview. You need to prepare yourself for all three types of interviews prior to your interview. Since the type of interview and possibly the number of interviewers are unknown, you will not be able to gauge the type of interview process until the beginning of the interview. By preparing for each type of interview, you can be aware of the direction of the interview as soon as it begins. In most interviews, you will initially be given information about the company and the role for which you are interviewing. At the end of each interview, regardless of how many participants there are in the interview, ask for the interviewers' contact information including email addresses, phone numbers, correct spelling of their names, and their titles — or just ask for their business cards.

1. *The formal interview* — The formal interview usually occurs with larger companies that have set guidelines for conducting an interview. Mid-size and small companies can also conduct a formal interview process. The formal interview is not as interactive or as personal

as the informal or unprepared interviews. The interviewers have a set list of questions they will ask, and they will give you a chance to respond. You will most probably be instructed to ask your questions at the end of the interview. The formal interview makes it difficult to develop a rapport with the interviewer and, honestly, it is designed that way. Listen carefully to the questions and adapt your tone and body language. If they are conducting a formal interview, make sure your responses are in the same tone as the interview. At the end of a formal interview you will probably be told that the company is interviewing several candidates, and they will contact you about any next steps. If they have not shared with you the next steps, you can ask about the timeline to hire. For example, when do they expect to finish this part of the interview process? How many more interviews will there be before a decision is made?

2. *The informal interview* — This interview is the most comfortable in the interview process. The interviewers have questions they want to ask and probably in no specific order. They will usually allow you to ask questions during the interview without going off track. You will be able to establish an initial rapport with the interviewer that will allow you to get a basic understanding of the person and what they are looking for in the interview. This initial small talk will set the tone for the entire interview. The informal interview is, in my opinion, the best way for you to get to know the company and for the company to understand your goals and work ethic. Don't become too relaxed during the interview. Don't let your guard down, as your interviewers are listening to your responses and will make their decision based upon the tone of your responses.

3. *The unprepared interview* — The unprepared interview is usually conducted by smaller companies that do not have a formal interview

process. You will be asked questions that are not planned or written down and in no specific order. In these interviews it can be difficult to gauge the tone or response of the interviewer, and it is important to stay focused. Always take on the tone of your interviewer. And as in the informal interview process, don't let your guard down, as there is usually a purpose behind the line of questioning. Due to the more relaxed tone and format, these interviews give you an opportunity to build yourself up and show the interviewer that you are the most qualified candidate for the position.

As I mentioned previously, before the interview has ended make sure you have the interviewers' contact information. Once you have completed the interview, prepare either an email or handwritten thank-you note to everyone with whom you interviewed. Send the note no more than twenty-four hours after the interview. If you are definitely interested in the position or if you think you might be interested (if the latter is the case, leave your options open for further discussion about the position!), let each of the interviewers know that you are excited about the opportunity and you are confident that you can be an asset to their organization. If you are certain that you are not interested in the position, you should send a note thanking the interviewers for their time and let them know this position is not right for you. Be professional and considerate. Always keep your options open, as another position may become available at this company.

After the interview you will always find something you could have said or could have added to your responses. We all get insecure after the interview process. Remember, what you could have said is not an issue, as you did the best you could. Don't second-guess yourself.

The interviewers' responses to you at the end of the interview is always interesting. We live in a litigious society, and most companies are sensitive about how they present themselves. They want to make sure everything they do is without discrimination or bias. So the responses you will get at the completion of an interview usually will tell you very little about how well you interviewed or when (and if) you will proceed to the next step. Occasionally, answers to your prepared questions will give you some insight into a possible next step in the interview process. I can't tell you how many times I have heard people say that they aced the interview and were just waiting for an offer letter. Most of these people will receive a letter thanking them for applying for the position and informing them that the company hired a more qualified candidate. Companies will not — and cannot — let you know that you did not do well in the interview or that they felt you were not qualified for the position. Most likely, you will leave the interview with no clear direction regarding next steps.

A few years ago when I was in the staffing business, I had a candidate interview for a position at an entertainment company as a programmer. The candidate called me after the interview to let me know he aced the interview, and my client had asked him to start on Monday morning. I was excited to learn that he was hired. I called my corporate client and asked how the interview went. He let me know in no uncertain terms that if I ever sent him a candidate like that again, he would no longer do business with me! I guess it just goes to show that some candidates can read way too much into an interviewer's purposefully neutral language such as, "Thank you; we'll be in touch." So I guess there are three sides to every story — the interviewer's, the candidate's, and the truth!

Interview and Pre-Interview Questions

In some instances a company will send you a list of questions to answer prior to being accepted for an interview with the hiring manager, interview team, or other decision makers. Although most of these questions are usually asked during an in-person or video interview there is always the chance the company may ask you to answer a few questions prior to your interview in a pre-interview questionnaire. These pre-interview questions are designed to eliminate candidate who are not qualified for the position. They are usually sent to you by email, and you will need to submit your answers promptly, so your interview can be scheduled with the decision makers.

There are two types of questions that you will be asked to answer in the pre-interview questionnaire as well as in your in-person or video interview with the decision makers:

- *Technical questions* — These questions will center around your technical ability to perform the job. Answer the questions to the best of your ability by researching your answers. If you are not sure of the answer even after conducting extensive research do not answer the question — don't guess. Unfortunately, this may preclude you from an interview, but an honest incorrect answer or a "no experience with this technology" answer is always the right thing to do. If, for example, you are a software engineer with a specific skill set and you are asked to answer a specific question about a software product of which you have limited exposure or no knowledge you can always answer by expressing your interest in learning more about the product. In some cases you might be given a scenario for a project assignment and asked how you would handle the project from start to finish. As a salesperson you may be asked to "sell" the company's product during the interview with a formal sales presentation. If the technical skill in question is part of your background and experience, make sure you answer thoroughly with specific examples. For sales and customer service roles some questions will center around your ability to work with the company's systems including the customer relationship management (CRM) platform. Technical questions are usually not asked when you are applying for an administrative position, however, certain tests may be administered to assess your knowledge of job-specific skills.

- *Behavioral questions* — These questions are designed to give the company a better understanding of how you will react in a specific situation. Questions are designed to understand how you will fit into the culture of the company. If you are applying for a management position, these questions are designed to see how you may react to a certain situation as a manager. For example, "As a manager you have two employees who are experiencing a conflict — how would you defuse the situation?" There are some behavioral questions that I consider "gotcha questions" or more bluntly "stupid interview questions." Be very careful how you answer these questions. In some cases the interviewers are looking for specific answers and, in other cases, they just want to see how you will react to a surprise question.

When it comes to in-person, video, and pre-interview questions that are considered behavioral, you could be given multiple questions spanning a wide variety of topics. Take time to answer each question honestly and be sure to stay on topic. Here are a few behavioral questions you could be asked:

1. "Tell me about yourself." — There are three kinds of answers to this question: a five-word answer, a two-sentence discussion, or everything you have ever done in your life. Be concise and keep your answer to just a few sentences by discussing your experience and how it relates to the company and the position. Make sure you give them just enough information to be interested in you. For example, you can address your personal goals and family, but shy away from discussing your hobbies and interests.

2. "What are your strengths?" — Note your accomplishments and your ability to get things done. For a management position explain how you built your team and created a positive work environment.

3. "What are your weaknesses?" — Be careful with this one. Try to spin this question to a positive by emphasizing what you have learned

and how you have improved in a work situation. Don't spend time on information that is negative.

4. "How long will it take you to contribute to our company?" — This is the time to put the question back on the company by asking them to clarify their expectations during your interview. Once, you get clarification in the interview you can easily answer this question.

5. "Give two examples of your creativity." — Prepare for this question and discuss your accomplishments and creative solutions.

6. "What are your salary/hourly expectations for this position?" — Be careful with your answer. In some states, the District of Columbia, and Puerto Rico, interviewers are prohibited from asking this question. See Appendix 1 for a list of states, counties, and municipalities that have enacted this prohibition. It is good to understand what you can and cannot be asked by a potential employer. If you are interviewing in any of these areas and you are asked this question about your salary expectations or salary history it is your decision on whether or not to answer it. This question is best answered during the interview by asking the interviewer about the salary range for the position. When answering pre-interview questions in writing, you could respond by saying, "Before we discuss salary, I would like to learn more about the position and the responsibilities, so we can have an open conversation during my interview about how I can be an asset to the organization." Or you can say, "I'd like to have an open and honest conversation about salary expectations and your salary range during my interview." If you state that you know it is illegal to ask about salary, you may run the risk of immediate disqualification from consideration for the position. Most companies have a salary range for positions they are looking to fill. If the salary range

is acceptable to you (see your Circle of Acceptance) let them know that this is in line with your career goals. By researching the company or by closely reviewing a job posting, website, or job board you can usually find out the salary/hourly rate they are expecting to pay. If the salary/hourly range is outside of your Circle of Acceptance, this is the time to let them know you will need to further discuss your background and experience. Later in the hiring process if you feel there is no room for negotiation, it is time to professionally let them know you are no longer interested in the position.

7. "Has there been a situation in which you were criticized for your work? How did you respond?" — Be specific and discuss how you responded in the most positive tone. Explain how you learned from the situation.

8. "Tell us about your previous employer." — Don't be negative! Share situations that were upbeat and positive. For example, "It is an excellent company, and I had many valuable experiences that have allowed me to learn and grow in my position." In some situations the interviewers know about your previous company and will ask you specific questions that may encourage you to give a negative response. Stay positive even when you are presented with negative comments.

9. "How long do you intend to stay with our company?" — This is a loaded question. The safe answer is that you are looking for a long-term career opportunity with advancement and growth. Many candidates are using a position as a stepping-stone to a better position. If you are in this category be careful with your response, as letting them know that this position is not a long-term commitment can eliminate any next steps for you in the process.

10. "Why should we hire you?" — Discuss your background and experience and how it relates to the position. Talk about your excitement about the position and the company. Let them know you are a team player, and you will have an immediate, positive impact in the department and the company. If you are interviewing for a managerial position, address your abilities to increase revenue, lower costs, and mentor a team.

Remember, these questions are simply the company's way to get as much information about you as possible prior to the interview. Technical questions assess your ability to do the job, and behavioral questions reveal your ability to adapt to the company's culture.

There are perhaps hundreds of sample interview questions. To prepare for the pre-interview questionnaire as well as for your in-person or video interview, I encourage you to review the interview questions in Appendix 2. This is structured as a worksheet, so you can spend time thinking about your answers prior to the interview process.

Your preparation for an interview is just as important as the interview itself. Sometimes the interviewer asks a question and expects a specific answer. You might call these trick questions, but the safest way to answer these questions is to give an answer that is genuine and authentic.

Don't answer the question based on what you think the interviewer wants to hear. The reason is simple. If you give an answer that is, in your opinion, what the interviewer wants to hear, I can almost guarantee that you will end up in a position that is not right for you. Be careful with your answers and answer honestly. A less-than-honest answer will always come back to haunt you after you accept the position.

You should have a clear understanding of your Interview Circle of Acceptance prior to the interview. If you feel that a completely honest answer would be a non-starter for the company, you need to refer to your Circle of Acceptance to clarify what is acceptable to you. If the answer is outside your Circle, then this may not be the position for you.

CIRCLE OF ACCEPTANCE
MY INTERVIEW

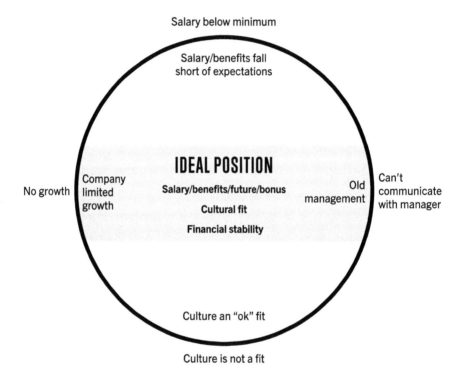

Salary below minimum

Salary/benefits fall
short of expectations

IDEAL POSITION

No growth | Company limited growth | **Salary/benefits/future/bonus** | Old management | Can't communicate with manager

Cultural fit

Financial stability

Culture an "ok" fit

Culture is not a fit

Let's continue our discussion about the salary or hourly question in those areas where it is still legal to have this conversation. As noted earlier, one interview question that is always difficult to answer is, "What salary/hourly wage are you expecting?" Of course in a few instances, the company will tell you they are offering a specific salary. (If the salary is outside your Circle of Acceptance, you can negotiate for a higher amount — we will discuss negotiations in the next chapter.) In many cases the interviewers will ask you what you are expecting. If your answer is too low, they may think you are not qualified for the position. If your answer is too high, you may disqualify yourself from further consideration.

The best way to answer this question is to answer it with a question! Instead of giving them a salary or hourly number or rate, ask about the salary range for this position. Most organizations have a range (low, medium, and high). Ideally, you have already designed your Circle of Acceptance, so when you are told the salary range you will know whether it is acceptable or unacceptable. If the salary is acceptable, let them know. However, if the top of the range is still below your point of acceptance, let them know the salary you were expecting by citing your past salary history. At this point if you are told that the top of the salary range is the maximum they could pay — and it is outside your Circle of Acceptance — you may need to end the interview.

But before you decide this is not the right position for you, you can discuss other negotiation options to consider making it a win/win.

- A company may be able to fast track your salary requirement during the first year. If this falls within your Circle of Acceptance, you will receive your desired salary.

- A company may be able to offer other perks such as increased benefits, additional vacation days, a sign-on bonus, additional paid time off (PTO), a car allowance, education reimbursement, stock options, working remotely, equity, and accelerated vesting. An unacceptable salary now becomes acceptable.

- But also be prepared for the interviewers to end the interview if you are asking for too much salary, and they feel you are not willing to negotiate.

I have had many experiences interviewing job seekers who ask for too little in salary or hourly wage and job seekers who ask for too much. Be careful not to fall into either of these categories. A few years ago I was recruiting for a company that was looking for a senior mechanical engineer. I asked a candidate what he made in his current position, and he told me he was being paid $75,000 annually. He mentioned that he would only accept a new position starting at $105,000 annually. That was a hefty increase, and I let him know he was asking for too much. He was firm with his requested salary and subsequently was not hired.

Conversely, I spoke with a more junior person who was asking for $10,000 a year lower than the low range of the salary. Most recruiters or managers would conclude that this person may not be qualified for the position based upon this low salary requirement. These examples illustrate why you should ask about the salary range. If, on the one hand, the salary range is within your Circle of Acceptance there is no need for further negotiations. On the other hand, if it is outside your Circle and not negotiable, it is probably time to seek out another company.

Tough Interview Questions

I have complied a list of some tough interview question for your review. I encourage you to take a moment to consider your answer to each of the following questions. In fact, you might want to jot down some thoughts, so you can be prepared with discussion points during your interview:

"Why are you leaving your current position?" — A very critical question. Don't say anything negative about your previous employer. Don't sound too opportunistic. It is also good to state that, after long personal consideration, the chance to contribute and grow at your current company is limited.

- "What do you consider to be your most significant accomplishment?" — This can get you the job. Prepare extensively by writing an outline of your accomplishments. Talk for no more than two minutes with details of your accomplishments and discuss personal involvement. If, for example, you have increased productivity by a certain percentage discuss the increase and how you made it happen.

- "Why do you believe you are qualified for this position?" — Pick two or three main factors about the job and about your experience that are most relevant. Discuss for two minutes with specific details. Select a technical skill, a specific management skill (organizing, staffing, planning), and a personal success.

- "Have you ever accomplished something you didn't think you could?" — This falls into the category of "stupid interview questions," because we all accomplish larger and larger projects as we grow in our careers. Simply provide a good example where you overcame numerous difficulties to succeed. Just show them you can do what is necessary — and beyond — to achieve the best possible result.

- "What do you like/dislike about your current position?" — Another "stupid interview question." The interviewer is trying to determine compatibility with the open position. Try to phrase everything in a positive light. Perhaps you don't like working overtime or project-completion pressure, but there is nothing wrong with liking challenges, pressure situations, and opportunity to grow or disliking bureaucracy and frustrating situations.

- "How do you handle pressure? Do you like or dislike these situations?" — This question may imply that the position is pressure packed and out of control. There is nothing wrong with this if you know what you're getting into. If you do perform well under stress, provide a good example with details by letting the interviewer "feel" the stress of your situation and how you achieved the "impossible." If you don't perform well in pressure situations you can ask questions about the position, so you will understand the level of pressure you will be experiencing in the job.

- "The sign of a good employee is the ability to take initiative. Can you describe situations like this about yourself?" — If you are a proactive, results-oriented person, you do not have to be told what to do or micro-managed. This is a success attribute. Provide a series of short examples describing your self-motivation. Try to discuss at least one example in-depth (no more than two minutes). Demonstrate your extra effort and strong work ethic.

- "What's the worst or most uncomfortable aspect of your career?" — And this is another "stupid interview question," because no job or career is perfect and you could accidentally reveal something embarrassing. This is a general question to learn about you. Also, they are looking to see if you can learn from your mistakes. If you can, it indicates that you are open and flexible. Don't be afraid to talk about your challenges, particularly if you've learned from them. Be very careful with your response. Try to place a positive light on any embarrassing or uncomfortable situation.

- "What do you consider to be your most significant strengths?" — Just be prepared. Be prepared to share four or five key elements of both your soft skills and technical strengths. Be able to discuss each with a specific example. Select those key elements that are specific to the job opening such as your ability to interact equally with superiors and peers, knowing when to make suggestions, and understanding how to complete a task.

- "What do you consider to be your most significant weaknesses?" — This is another example of a "gotcha" question. Don't reveal any part of your life that is too personal or embarrassing. Try to communicate your response in a positive light. Rather, discuss weaknesses that you have changed over a period of time. For example, you have had challenges with making oral presentations, but you have taken the time to become an excellent presenter by joining a Toastmasters group.

- "How do you handle multiple deadlines and difficult people?" — Most companies experience these problems daily. You need to show the interviewer that you can deal with these day-to-day issues by offering solutions rather than getting caught up in corporate politics. Show how your diplomacy and patience allow you to overcome these everyday situations. Discuss your ability to prioritize your assigned tasks.

- "How do you compare your technical skills to your management skills?" — You will need to balance this answer if you want to be considered for a managerial position. Managers tend to minimize their technical skills, because they don't have a depth of technical skills, or their technical skills are not up to date, or they are not a hands-on manager. Most successful managers possess an excellent balance between managing people and understanding the technical aspects of their position. Share how you have been successful in these areas with a short story on how you managed both successfully.

- "How would you handle a situation with tight deadlines, low employee morale, and inadequate resources?" — The best way to address this question is with an example. Discuss your toughest management task, even if it is outside the job description. To be an effective project manager, team leader, or supervisor you need to possess organizational and interpersonal skills. Your ability to answer these questions will indicate the level of your management experience.

- "Are you satisfied with your career to date? What would you change if you could?" — Be honest and genuine in your response. The interviewer wants to know if you are going to be happy in the position. Don't spend too much time talking about your career mistakes. Put a positive tone on the changes you have made throughout your career. If you are transitioning your career, let the interviewer know that your choice has been well thought out and you will be an asset to the company.

- "What are your career goals? Where do you see yourself five years from now?" — Most importantly, be realistic! I am sure that most of us would like to answer this question by saying, "I want your job!" Instead, talk about growing with the company and making a positive impact in your role. Perhaps discussing a goal of up to three promotions in the next five years is a good first step.

- "Why should we hire you for this position?" — This is a good chance to summarize by being assertive and not aggressive. Don't be cocky. Restate highlights and show how your experience will bring the best practices you have learned to the new role by citing a few of your successes. You will need to demonstrate a thoughtful, organized, strong effort and positive attitude.

As a reminder, Appendix 2 contains a worksheet with additional interview questions. As noted earlier, I encourage you to spend time considering your answer to each question to prepare for your interview. Expect the unexpected — preparation is the key to a successful interview.

How Long Is The Typical Interview?

The length of the interview can tell you everything you may need to know about the interview process. You may be told that the interview will last twenty minutes. In a formal interview you might not have an opportunity to ask questions, and the interviewer will let you know that they will reach out to you in the next week. In this case they have scheduled only twenty minutes as this may be a requirement of their company.

In an informal interview they may have allotted twenty or thirty minutes for the interview. What if they only ask a few questions and then abruptly end the interview? This could be a red flag, as they may have subjectively decided you may not be the right fit for the position. Of course, they will let you know that you will be hearing from them in the next few days or a week. However, there may have been something that was said, viewed, or inferred that made the interviewer think that you are not the person for the position.

These are the parts of the interview you cannot control. You have done all your pre-interview preparation, but there may be one minor "blip" in your answers that made the interviewer think you were not qualified for the position. Remember, you can only control what you have prepared for and the specific answers you gave or perhaps something you were wearing can prompt the interviewer to abruptly end the interview. If the interview is ended before the allotted time, don't let this get you down, as the reasons were out of your control.

Some interviewers will develop an opinion about you in the first five minutes. I have conducted hundreds of interviews, and I have abruptly ended the interview because the first impression was negative. In these instances I knew that, regardless of their qualification, the candidate was not the right fit for the position. Don't obsess about an interview that is abruptly ended, as there was nothing you could have done to change the interviewer's perception of you. The interviewer may have determined you do not have the technical skills for the position or you may not be a cultural fit. Perhaps he or she did not like the sound of your voice or how you were dressed, or perhaps the interviewer was in a foul mood. All of these examples are out of your control!

Telephone Interviews

The telephone interview is the most difficult component of the interview process. Yes, you have performed all the pre-interview research including viewing the interviewers' LinkedIn profiles. By conducting your research about the company and the interviewers, you have now created a level of comfort, and that is a great start! It is important to be extremely focused during a telephone interview. When the interview is being scheduled always ask the scheduler how many people (and their titles) will be involved in the interview. Again, by asking this question you avoid any surprises when the interview begins.

- If you have a landline, use it. If you are using a mobile phone, make sure you have a strong connection. Although it is no one's fault if there is a poor connection, the cutting in and out on a mobile phone during a telephone interview is a negative.

- Situate yourself in a place where you cannot be interrupted. Background noise such as barking dogs, your children running in and out of the room, or a busy coffeeshop can possibly disqualify you from a position.

- Sit or stand in a comfortable place. Some people are more comfortable standing when they talk, so situate yourself in any position in which you are comfortable. But don't get too relaxed! Even though they cannot see you, the tone of your voice will be noticed if you are too comfortable or too rigid.

- If possible, sit at your computer and have the job description displayed on the screen with paper copies of your resume and interview questions easily accessible. If you are not at your computer have paper copies of the job description, your resume, and your interview questions nearby, so you can refer to them and make notes during the interview.

- When you are speaking (and I know this sounds silly) smile! The tone of your voice and the excitement for the position will be noticed by the interviewers. Also, as you answer questions try not to speak in a monotone — have excitement in your voice, and it will be noticed by the interviewers.

- As your telephone interview is coming to an end make sure you ask your prepared questions. Have the questions in front of you through-out the interview, so if they have already answered your question, don't ask it again. Take this time to let them know how interested you are in the position. If, however, you don't feel that this is the right job for you, let them know and thank them for their time.

- And perhaps most importantly allow the interviewers to ask the questions. Don't interrupt the interviewers — let them finish asking their question before you respond.

If you are interested in moving forward in the interview process after the telephone interview, ask about the next steps. Here are some questions you can ask:

- Will there be an in-person or video interview?

- How soon do they want to fill this position?

- If you are comfortable with the interviewers, you can ask how many candidates they will interview and their thoughts about your expe-rience and background as it relates to the position. Be careful with this question, as it should only be asked if you are comfortable with the conversation.

- Ask whether this opportunity is a new position or replacement position. If it is a replacement, you can ask why the last person is no longer with the company. Don't be afraid to ask if there are any internal candidates being considered. These types of questions validate that this is YOUR INTERVIEW — you have a right to know. Be aware that some interviewers may not answer this question or may be offended by the question. If this is the case, it can give you a clearer picture of the company culture and the management style. You will then need to decide if you want to move the interview process to the next step.

- Thank them for their time and make sure you have their contact information.

Regardless of the type of interview, it's important to send a handwritten thank-you note or an email thanking them for their time no more than twenty-four hours after the interview. Don't hesitate to express your interest in the position by stating that you are confident you will be an asset to the organization.

The telephone interview is the precursor to either an in-person or a video interview. Each part of the interview process is as important as the next. Stay focused, remain on subject, and always expect the unexpected. By researching the company and reviewing the profiles of all the people who are interviewing you, you will be prepared.

Regardless of the company or the hiring process, it has been my experience that for most mid-size and large companies, hiring is not a priority! Sure, they have a job that needs to be filled, but the day-to-day responsibilities of management and moving their company forward will always take precedence. So if you are told they will respond to you in a week or so, you might expect that it will be two weeks or more. The time lapse does not mean you are not in consideration for the position. It is simply a matter of company priorities. To that end, make sure you stay ahead of the situation by reaching out to the company in a professional manner. Be assertive about your interest in the position, but don't be aggressive! If, for example, you have been told that they will respond to you in a week — and if you have not heard from them in ten days — write a short email letting the employer know that you remain interested in the position. By doing this you will keep your name visible to the company and will be a continued part of the decision-making process. By failing to reach out to the company, the company may think you are not interested in the position.

What's next? You have aced your telephone interview, and now it's time to meet in person.

In-Person Interviews

In-person interviews have been the norm for meeting prospective employees. The COVID-19 pandemic changed the interview process, and video interviews are becoming the new normal. Many companies have embraced this shift and will continue to conduct their interviews with prospective candidates by video, because it is a relatively easy, efficient process. That said, it is still important to understand the in-person interview.

You have successfully completed the telephone interview, and you have been asked to meet the company representative (or several representatives) in person. Or possibly the company has asked you for an in-person interview without an initial telephone interview. You have researched the company and have been given a date and time for the interview. You have prepared by asking how long the interview will last, who will be interviewing you, and you understand the company dress code. You are ready to take the next step. You have your written list of questions that you will ask during the interview. (Remember that none of these questions should be directly related to salary, benefits, or time off.) And most importantly, you know that this is YOUR INTERVIEW!

The in-person interview could be the final step before you are offered a position with the company you have chosen. You are nervous, you want the job, and you want to do everything possible to make sure you make a great impression. You have prepared, so don't overthink the process. We all have those thoughts that get into our heads such as, "What if I don't answer the questions the way they want me to answer them? Will they like me? Am I confident enough to get through the interview?"

You have prepared for everything you can expect, and rest assured that you will be given a question or a situation that you are not prepared for — don't make this an issue. It is YOU who will decide whether you want the job. Remember, they are going to hire someone with your qualifications and background. If it is you, it is your choice to accept or decline the position.

There will be factors that qualify or disqualify you from a position. Know what you can control, and be aware of those factors you cannot control. For example, you can control the tone of the interview by being prepared, asking questions, and being positive. You cannot control how you are seen by the interviewer. Unfortunately, I have seen some interviewers disqualify a person, because they did not like the colors they were wearing! As much as we would like to think that the interview process is objective, it is not. The technical portion of the interview is, for the most part, objective. As the interview process segues to assessing your behavioral make-up, the interview is quite subjective.

As an interviewer and interviewee, I have found that a good percentage of people will make up their mind about you in the first ten minutes of the interview. If you have done your research and prepared all that you can control, you have done your job in getting ready for the interview.

Use this checklist to prepare for your interview:

- Confirm the time and date of the interview.

- Use the Internet or GPS to discover the fastest route to the office where you will be interviewed.

- If the interview location is more than twenty minutes from your home or current office, take time to make a practice trip to the site. Note that as much as you may prepare, outside influences may cause a delay to your arrival time such as traffic accidents. If one of these outside influences causes you to be delayed on the day of your interview, call the company and let them know you will be late — don't just show up ten minutes late and expect everything to be OK.

- On the day of the interview prepare by going over your questions, taking another look at the company website, and reviewing the profiles of the interviewer or interviewers. Reread your resume including any gaps in your work history — practice your answers to address these gaps. And definitely reread the job description.

- Dress appropriately — usually one step up from the day-to-day dress code of the company.

- Show up for the interview on "Vince Lombardi time." That is to say, arrive for the interview at least ten minutes early but not more than twenty minutes before the interview. Arriving too early can give the impression that you are a bit too anxious.

- Even in today's digital world take a notepad, a pen, and four paper copies of your resume as well as any information the company may have asked you to bring to the interview. I know resume paper copies appear to be a thing of the past, but it is wise to have these four copies with you in a manila envelope, because it may be helpful to hand them out to multiple interviewers. Some companies will send you an application and other pertinent information to complete prior to the interview, so include these papers in your manila envelope.

- If you smoke (anything) refrain from doing so before the interview. I can guarantee that the odor will be noticeable.

- When meeting interviewers, shake their hands with a firm (not tight) handshake. Make eye contact. I have conducted hundreds of interviews, and I have seen many people who cannot maintain eye contact with the interviewer. If you know it is difficult for you to make eye contact, practice with a family member or a friend prior to the interview. Not making eye contact can be a non-starter for many interviewers.

- If you are escorted to the interviewer's office, make sure you are aware of the surroundings. Are there pictures on the wall or their desk, are there trophies and commendations? As we've discussed, you can learn about the person who is interviewing you in just a few seconds, and this could possibly give you a chance to ask them about their family and their interests. This kind of conversation icebreaker can take the initial edge off the beginning of the inter-view. You will probably be asked to sit in a chair opposite the desk or at a small conference table in the office. Sit upright but not stiff, and don't become too relaxed. I remember walking into the office of the director for a government agency and saw a picture of a golf course I had just played. I made a short comment that it was one of the best and most beautiful courses in the country, and just that simple comment opened our conversation to levels I never would have expected.

- If you are escorted to a conference room, you will be directed to sit in a particular spot that is comfortable for them. If the interview is with one person, make sure you make eye contact throughout the interview. If there are multiple interviewers, make sure you introduce yourself to each person with the same firm (but not tight) handshake and, during the interview, make eye contact with each interviewer as you answer his or her question.

- You will almost immediately be able to determine the type of interview: formal, informal, or unprepared. You will need to adapt to the interviewer's style and tone and the type of interview.

- Answer all the questions with complete and substantive responses. Stay on subject and always respond with truthful answers. If you don't know the answer to a question, ask the interviewer to clarify the question. Trying to answer any questions without knowing the answer may disqualify you from the position. If you don't know the answer, let them know this and, if possible, tell the interviewer you are a quick learner and you are almost sure to know the answer in a short period of time.

Now that the interview is coming to an end, be sure to address these details:

- Remember to thank all interviewers for their time, and express that you are extremely interested in the position. If you are!

- If you did not already ask this question, you can ask how many candidates they will be interviewing and ask them to share their thoughts about your experience and background as it relates to the position. Be careful with this question, as it should only be asked if you are comfortable with the conversation.

- If you do not know whether this position is a new position or a replacement position — or if there are any internal candidates — you can ask this question now. If it is a replacement position, you can ask why the last person is no longer with the company. Again, these types of questions validate that this is YOUR INTERVIEW — you have a right to know. Be aware that some interviewers may not answer this question or may be offended by the question.

- Ask about the next steps in the process.

- If you are comfortable with the interviewer or interviewers you can ask where the company is in the interview process and when you can expect to hear from them.

- Make sure you have each person's contact information, so you can send a handwritten thank-you note or an email.

- If you are not interested in the position, gracefully let them know that you appreciate the time they have taken to interview you but that you feel this is not the right position for you.

- As you are leaving, shake their hands with a firm handshake.

The in-person interview is your time to tout your personality and your ability to do the job. There is a fine line between talking about your accomplishments and being so self-centered that you do not consider the people who are conducting the interview. Always be aware of the people you are speaking with and consider that they have an interview process they are completing.

The secret to a successful in-person interview is understanding your audience and adapting your responses to them. I have conducted many interviews where the person I am interviewing becomes so self-absorbed that they do not consider the interviewer. By listening and responding with answers that are specific and on subject, you will complete a successful interview.

The in-person interview may have met its match with the onset of COVID-19. The virus has virtually changed the way we do everything. I am convinced that video interviews will become the new norm.

Video Interviews

During the COVID-19 pandemic, companies dramatically increased their use of video interviews in place of in-person interviews. As we continue to see further growth in technology and the vast improvement in conducing video conferences, I believe the video interview will be an additional or replacement step in the interviewing process. It could become a preview to an in-person interview, or it will simply replace the in-person interview.

I remember participating in a video interview in 1997. Suffice to say technology has evolved! In the 1990s there was a six-second delay when answering or asking a question. Talk about an uncomfortable environment — that was perhaps one of the most difficult job interviews I have experienced. I was offered the job, but I turned it down!

Virtually all the steps we discussed for an in-person interview remain the same for a video interview. You will need to prepare your questions, be present on the video interview at least three to four minutes before the start of the interview (you want to make sure your Internet connection is working and strong), dress appropriately, and most importantly remember — THIS IS YOUR INTERVIEW!

There are, however, additional preparations you will need to accomplish prior to a video interview:

- Test your Internet connection to ensure the interview can be conducted without interruption. A poor connection is a red flag for some interviewers. If your connection is weak, contact your Internet provider to ensure a secure and good connection.

- Use a computer or a tablet for a video interview. Do not use a mobile phone. If you do not have a computer, buy one, rent one, or borrow one. Using a mobile phone for a video interview can be distracting and inconsistent. I have conducted coaching sessions with clients who use their mobile phones for our sessions. My experience is that it is quite frustrating, since the screen is rarely stable. Even though there are stands that stabilize a mobile phone, I would still recommend using a computer or tablet. For a coaching session I can deal with the movement of the screen, but for an interview this could create a negative impression of you.

- Have all research material about the company and the interviewers along with your questions readily available for easy access during the interview. Searching for your interview questions or not knowing everything you can about the interviewers and the position can have you scrambling for answers.

- Eliminate any possible distractions, so the interviewer can concentrate on you. Find a room or a place that has no fancy backdrops, posters, pictures, or political statements in the background. If possible, create a white background (for example, a clean and ironed bed sheet or a large white board). Anything that may distract the interviewer can possibly be a reason for disqualification — remember you can control what they see. Some video conferencing software will allow you to choose your background. Make sure the background is benign so as not to cause any additional distractions. For example, no pictures of your hobbies, yourself, or your family.

- Be sure you have adequate lighting. Don't have the sun shining on your computer or have the room too dark.

- If you have a mobile phone or a landline in the room, make sure the ringer is turned off, so you and the interviewers are not distracted.

- There are several platforms for a video conference. Prior to the interview make sure you have installed the specific software for the video interview on your computer. Test the sound on your computer or tablet prior to the interview.

- If there are other people in your home or office, inform them that you are not to be disturbed during the interview for any reason. If you have pets, make sure they are not present in the room during the interview, and do everything possible to ensure no barking dogs. I have had numerous instances during video interviews and coaching sessions where someone is lurking in the background, folding laundry, or talking to someone else. I even had a person in the background flush the toilet during the video conference! Suffice to say, be alone during the interview.

- The cameras on computers are tricky at best. You can look at the camera, and it might appear to the interviewers that you are not looking at the screen or at them. Or you might be looking at the screen, and the camera may show your profile differently. Prior to the interview, practice using your computer camera to figure out what you should be looking at — the camera or the screen. If you are unable to accomplish this prior to the interview just look directly into the screen.

- If you are not familiar with video interviewing, you may become distracted by seeing your image on the screen. Sometimes we like what we see, and sometimes we don't! In order to eliminate some of the stress factors, take time to practice how you present yourself, perhaps with a friend or family member. If you are not comfortable with the technology, the interviewers might assume that you are not comfortable with the interview.

- As we discussed in the section on telephone interviews, you need to sit in a comfortable position — not too stiff or too relaxed. This is magnified ten-fold in a video interview.

- During the in-person interview you need to be animated and attentive — this also applies to the video interview. If you are undisturbed, you can pay full attention to the interviewers and their questions.

- Just as with all other types of interviews, as the interview is coming to an end, be sure to thank the interviewers for their time and let them know you are extremely interested in the position (if you are). Here are a few important reminders:

  - Ask if they can share the next steps in the interviewing process. For example, "Will there be an additional interview? How soon are you expecting to extend an offer?" If you are comfortable with the interviewer or interviewers, you can ask where they are in the interview process and when you can expect to hear from them.

  - Make sure you have all the interviewers' contact information, so you can send a handwritten thank-you note or email within twenty-four hours.

  - If you are not interested in the position, gracefully let them know that you appreciate the time they have taken to interview you, but you feel this is not the right position for you.

Automated Video Interviews

I have recently encountered a different type of video interview. A few large companies are now conducting an initial *automated* video interview, which only asks questions for the candidate to answer. You are required to be in front of your computer, dressed appropriately, and click the link for the video conference where you will be asked a series of prerecorded questions. Your responses will be timed, so make sure you are prepared to respond to the questions without hesitation. Your answers will be evaluated (perhaps by a person or perhaps by artificial intelligence software), and a decision will be made whether to allow you to move to the next step in the interview process.

In my opinion, this is the final step in taking the *personal* out of *personnel!* Employment with a chosen company is not only about your work product but also about human interaction. Of course, your selection for employment with a company is based upon both objective and subjective factors. This type of interview does not give you the ability to adapt to your audience, nor does it allow you to understand how the company works. You will not have the means to ask questions or find out anything more about the company. OK, enough of my opinion! This step in the interview process may be here to stay, so let's discuss how to make the most of this type of interview.

As we discussed in the chapter on networking, finding out about the company and the company culture is an important step for you to make the right decision about your career or your career transition. If you are faced with this automated video format to move forward in the interview process, accept it but, as we discussed earlier, prepare by knowing the company, understanding that this is both a technical and behavioral interview.

The technical portion will probably include questions dealing with your ability to do the job and may specifically ask you questions about how your background will be a value-add to the company. The behavioral part of the interview will revolve around your facial expressions, your reactions to the questions and, of course, how you answer the questions. Answer the questions honestly, and don't try to answer these questions with what you think the company wants to hear. Be honest, be straightforward, and let the company know how you can be an asset to them.

The interview is one of the final steps to beginning your new career or position. But it is not the last step in the process. So far you have chosen the company, you have successfully networked with the company representatives, and you have a clear understanding of the company culture. Your research, resume, networking, and your interviewing skills have resulted in a successful interview.

Congratulations, the company has made you an offer, and now you are on to the next, final steps. If the offer is made verbally, don't hesitate to ask for a written offer that details the terms of your employment. It's important to get all the details in writing including salary, benefits, and any negotiated points such as bonuses, additional PTO, or commissions.

Once the offer letter is received, it is your option to accept or reject the offer. Refer to the following Circle of Acceptance. If there are issues with your offer — for example, the salary is not what you expected, the benefits are less than you were told, or the position is not exactly what you were anticipating — you have an opportunity to negotiate your position, your salary, and your benefits.

The interview went well, and you are excited about working with this company. And now it is time to make sure this is the right position and you will receive the salary and benefits that are in your Circle of Acceptance.

CIRCLE OF ACCEPTANCE
POSITION OFFER

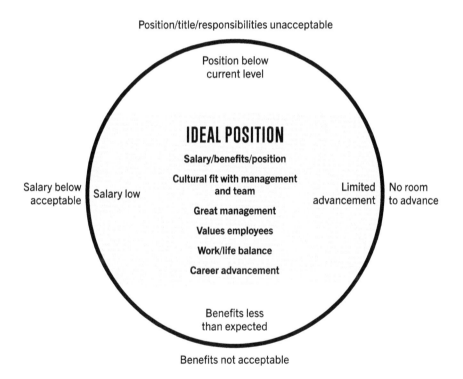

Position/title/responsibilities unacceptable

Position below
current level

IDEAL POSITION

Salary/benefits/position

**Cultural fit with management
and team**

Great management

Values employees

Work/life balance

Career advancement

Salary below
acceptable

Salary low

Limited
advancement

No room
to advance

Benefits less
than expected

Benefits not acceptable

CHAPTER 8
Negotiating Your Position, Salary, and Benefits

THE SECRET OF NEGOTIATION is to know that if you do not get what you want, you can walk away. That may sound harsh, however, if you accept a position that is not in your Circle of Acceptance all things that are job related will suffer. Almost immediately you will second-guess your decision. Once you begin the job you might start looking around for something better, and your work productivity might suffer. If you accept a position that is outside your Circle, there is a good chance you will regret this decision.

In dozens of offers that I have made to candidates many of them have accepted a salary or benefits package that they considered too low. Each person approached me after a short period of time saying that they needed to be paid more or they needed more benefits. Perhaps a bit cold but my response was always that they had accepted the position with the stated pay (or benefits package), and when it was time for their review I would consider their request for an increase. If they had attempted to negotiate their salary or benefits package initially, I may have been able to accommodate their request. Unfortunately, very few of these people remained employed. Often, their attitude suffered — and their work suffered. That is what happens when you don't negotiate and just accept what is offered if the offer is not acceptable to you.

Years ago I was working for a large staffing firm and was hiring a team to build a new division. A person who worked for another department in the company was interested in working for my technical division. We met for an interview, and I was impressed with this candidate's background and assertiveness. After thirty minutes or so, I asked how much he wanted to be compensated. I had interviewed over twenty other candidates for various positions around the country for this division, and I was able to offer salaries ranging from $50,000 to $75,000 annually. The candidate did not ask me about the salary range and was obviously unaware of the amount I could offer. This candidate immediately answered my question, letting me know that his minimum salary requirement was a $45,000 base salary. He left up to $30,000 on the table! I smiled (inside), and without hesitation I accepted that amount and made the offer on the spot. There was no negotiation and no questions about how much he could make after six months or a year. This is a perfect example of a candidate not researching the job or questioning the salary range. Nevertheless, I made the offer at $45,000 annually. Had he questioned the range or prepared for the interview, he could have made substantially more in the first year. This candidate became disgruntled with the low pay and soon moved on to a different position.

Another employee came to me on his three-month anniversary, wanting a higher salary. I informed him that he needed to be employed with the company for one year before we could review his salary. His response was shocking! He said he had not been working hard for the past three months because he was not being paid enough, and if he were given an increase in his base salary he would work harder. I was not only shocked but upset! Within two weeks he was terminated from the position.

So let's talk about how you can negotiate to ensure salary, benefits, and other important points that are within your Circle of Acceptance. You have interviewed with the company for your dream job and your chosen career. You have received a formal offer. Make sure you get your offer in writing, as I have seen too many times a company will formally offer a salary and benefits package that is quite different from the verbal offer. If the offer falls within your Circle of Acceptance, you are on your way to the onboarding process and days away from your first day on the job.

If, however, during the final stages of the interview or upon receipt of a written offer you find that this career opportunity falls outside your Circle of Acceptance, you will need to attempt to negotiate the salary, benefits, and other perks that you need to make this job experience acceptable to you. I strongly suggest you use the Circle of Acceptance presented in the previous chapter to understand what you need to negotiate, so all the details regarding this position are acceptable to the company and most importantly to you!

If you determine that the offer of employment is outside your Circle of Acceptance you will now need to negotiate certain parts of the offer, so you are comfortable accepting the offer. Create a list of the areas that fall outside your Circle and be prepared to discuss each item clearly, objectively, and unemotionally. Sometimes, as you negotiate and learn additional details about the offer, you may find that those parts of your employment offer that initially were unacceptable to you now fall within your Circle of Acceptance. If the salary, benefits, and so forth are now in your Circle, you can now accept the position without any reservation.

It is logical to assume that a company will make an offer that is, what they believe, the lowest offer you will accept (in line with current market rates). Every company has budget constraints and profit goals and does not want to expend more resources than necessary. We can also assume you will want to negotiate the highest possible salary in line with your experience. If these critical aspects of the position are not within your Circle of Acceptance, you can:

- Let the company know that the salary or benefits offered is not in the range you were anticipating. Try not to give them an exact figure — let them respond. If you do state your desired salary, you have locked yourself into a rate and there will be no further negotiation. But once they give you a new, specific salary, you will know if it is acceptable. Remember, knowing your audience (the company and the interviewers) is the best way to determine if you can negotiate for a larger increase. During the negotiation discussion be aware of the facial expressions, tone of voice, and body movements of the interviewers. If the new figure is acceptable to you, you can say "yes" and move to the next step in the hiring process. If, however, you feel that this is the most they will offer and it still falls outside your Circle of Acceptance, it may be time to walk away.

- If the company is not a large organization with strict policies about benefits and salary, you can more easily discuss your needs with them. Most small to mid-size companies can make adjustments to your salary and benefits including more vacation time, some assistance in matching your benefit payments, and an increase in the salary offered. Or if your position is a critical skill set (for example, a software developer with a highly specific discipline), you will have the ability to negotiate your terms.

- If the company offers you a salary that is below your acceptable range but offers an aggressive path to salary increases in an accelerated period (in writing), you will need to consider how soon you can achieve your salary goals. This path could move the offer back into your Circle of Acceptance. There are many perks a company can offer that can bring a position that has fallen outside your Circle of Acceptance back inside the Circle such as:

- Salary review within three or six months

- Promotion review within the first year

- Company retirement programs including a matching contribution

- Additional vacation time or paid time off (PTO)

- Remote work a few days a week (unless the work is 100 percent remote)

- Additional benefits including matching your healthcare premium payments or free healthcare

- Sign-on bonus

- Tuition reimbursement

- Stock options or equity (accelerated vesting in the company)

- Car allowance

- Year-end bonus

Negotiation is difficult for many people. Just like the interview you may feel that this is the only position available, and you don't want to walk away from the offer. It is important that you do not get caught in this mindset! Don't feel like you have to accept a company's offer, because you are not sure you can find another position. Or perhaps you might have convinced yourself that you simply don't want to go through this process again. Remember, this is your CAREER — it's not just a job! If this offer is not acceptable to you, be confident that in the immediate future there will be more interviews and more job offers that fall within your Circle of Acceptance. I know it is hard to anticipate your future, but accepting an offer that is outside your Circle will ensure two unacceptable outcomes:

- You will be seeking another position in a very short period (perhaps three or six months).

- You will look back thirty or forty years from now and say, "What was I thinking?" (I know I did.) Remember, It's Your Career — It's Your Choice!

Remember, accepting a position that is outside your Circle may cause you to be unhappy with your position. You may find yourself looking for another opportunity soon after you begin. Find and accept the position you want — not the one you may think you have to take just because an offer of employment was made. There is so much in your life that you cannot control. There are so many roadblocks that you will experience in every aspect of your life that you cannot anticipate. Make your career or your career transition a researched and calculated choice. Then, as you begin to set your retirement date in the years to come, you can look back on your career knowing you have made the right decisions.

CHAPTER 9
Working Remotely and the Hybrid Workforce

THE MAKE-UP OF THE WORKFORCE started undergoing a drastic change at the onset of the COVID-19 pandemic. In an incredibly short timeframe the labor force saw a dramatic increase in the number of employees working remotely. While the concept of telecommuting has been around for years, it was rarely viewed by employers as a productive business practice. March 2020 changed so much! Remote work became a necessity — and not an exception — as the pandemic demonstrated that much more work could be done remotely than previously thought.

As the pandemic abated, many companies began requiring their employees to return to the physical workspace. The reasons cited included these beliefs:

- More effective and productive work is accomplished when you are face-to-face with your peers.

- The onsite work environment creates a social atmosphere for employees, allowing them to become more balanced and effective.

- While the technology to host and attend virtual meetings and events has evolved, many positions — such as sales — require continual interaction with the public. For certain types of jobs, nothing can take the place of a face-to-face meeting.

Clearly, remote work is here to stay, and it can be accomplished without a loss of productivity. At the time of this writing, approximately 30 to 35 percent of the workforce works from home three to five days a week. This is a huge increase over the percentages in 2019. Business experts suggest that these percentages will remain stable for the foreseeable future. As technology advances we could see a rise in remote work, but this steady increase will not parallel the dramatic increase we saw during the height of the pandemic.

Many employers are developing remote work strategies for the long term to attract highly qualified talent who do not live locally. Of course, the employers must first determine whether the workers' activities can be done remotely without the loss of productivity. Plus, some employees don't want to work onsite, while many others prefer working in an office environment.

Many mid-size and large employers have adopted a hybrid model for this changing workforce. Many employees work onsite, and others work remotely for part of the week or the entire week. In many instances, employers are giving employees a choice to work onsite or remotely.

Once you receive an offer for a position with a company that has a hybrid workforce, you will have to decide what is best for you. There are pros and cons about working remotely just as there are pros and cons for working onsite.

Let's Look at Some Pros and Cons for Working Onsite:

Pros
- You interact directly with your peers and supervisors.
- You can get immediate feedback on questions and decisions.

- You have IT support onsite.
- In-person meetings are extremely productive.
- You can enjoy collaboration and the ability to learn from your peers.
- You have a venue for social interaction.

Cons

- Travel time to the worksite.
- Inability to set your schedule. (You will need to adhere to a specific daily schedule such as 8:00 a.m. to 5:00 p.m.)
- There are company politics including social mores such as how you dress, speak, or your overall demeanor.
- In a hybrid environment you must interact with remote workers.

Consider These Pros and Cons for Working Remotely:

Pros

- Your work environment is protected, comfortable, and safe.
- You don't have to dress up for work.
- No daily travel time to the worksite (save money on transportation).
- Less involvement in company politics.
- You can be more productive due to fewer interruptions from coworkers.

Cons

- Little daily interaction with peers and supervisors means fewer opportunities for high-energy, ad hoc brainstorming and collaboration. (Today's technology and video conferences cannot take the place of face-to-face meetings.)
- Working remotely can become very lonely and isolated.
- You are usually the last one to be made aware of company changes and may feel out of the loop when it comes to company communication.

- You may become less productive, because you can be distracted by personal issues, family members, and pets.
- Work/life balance can be extremely difficult to maintain. (Working remotely requires a great deal of discipline to be productive during normal business hours while not working in the evenings and weekends when your office is just a few steps away.)

Finally, this metamorphosis to a hybrid workforce is not clearly defined. We are currently experiencing the collision of four generations of workers in the workforce: Baby Boomers, Generation X, Generation Y (Millennials), and Generation Z. There are conflicting methods of work models and management styles, which can impact a company's current and future policies regarding a hybrid work environment. Over the next five to ten years, we may see a more defined business model for the hybrid workforce. As a job seeker, this changing environment can put you in the driver's seat, since you may be able to negotiate specific job requirements if you prefer to work remotely or onsite.

CHAPTER 10
Your Onboarding Experience

CONGRATULATIONS! Your research, networking, and resume have landed you an interview, and you aced it. You have received an offer for the position and the salary that is in your Circle of Acceptance. Most companies will present you with an offer letter outlining your salary, position, benefits, and a booklet of company policies (although most policies are boilerplate, make sure you read the entire pamphlet). Remember, no surprises! The offer letter will most probably be conditional upon your ability to pass a background check and possibly a drug screen.

Further, you will be asked to furnish a list of references. When supplying your new company with references make sure to do the following:

- Contact each reference and receive their permission to give the company their name and contact information.

- Speak to your references about the kind of reference they will give you. If it is not overly positive, don't use them.

- If you are asked to give a professional reference, the best reference to give is a former supervisor or manager. If the reference you give is a former coworker, ask this person to be very positive about your work product and mention that you got along well with other coworkers. Let them know the name of the company and the position you are accepting.

- If you are asked to give a personal reference, the best reference is someone you know well such as a friend or close neighbor. Try to stay away from giving personal references who do not know you well (for example, a banker, your pharmacist, or someone who just knows you in passing).

Part of your pre-employment process is to undergo a background check and possibly a drug screen. If there is something — anything — in your background that may be negative (for example, a misdemeanor including a DUI, a felony, or issues with your credit) tell the company about these issues before they begin the process of checking your background. I have seen numerous times where a company makes an offer and, after completing the background check, rescinds the offer due to a negative discovery. I once placed a candidate who was offered a position, but he forgot to tell me or the company he was convicted of grand theft auto over ten years ago. I am sure you can guess that the offer was rescinded.

As with your resume and interview be honest. I can assure you that a statement or an action that is negative in your background and has not been revealed to the company could possibly disqualify you from a position.

Drug tests have become standard in the pre-employment process. If you do not have any exposure to drugs, then there will be no issues. If, however, you have had exposure to drugs, make sure you are drug free for at least seven days prior to the test. For example, don't eat a poppy-seed muffin on the day of your drug screen! Yet be aware that some drug tests can detect a substance in your system for months. If you have been prescribed a prescription that may be detected in a drug screen, you will need to ask the onboarding specialist if that drug can be detected. By letting the company know you have a prescription there will be no surprises.

During the onboarding process you will be asked to fill out a variety of forms. You may be asked to select from a group of healthcare plans. Without delay, fill out these forms and return them to the company in a timely manner. If you are asked to select a healthcare plan and you are not familiar with these plans, don't hesitate to ask questions about the differences in the plans.

In addition, most mid-size and large companies offer choices for their retirement savings plans such as a 401(k) plan or matching plan. Again, if you are not sure of the best plan for you, either ask the onboarding specialist or consult your financial advisor.

You have now passed both your drug screen and your background check. You have been given a start date with the time and day you are to begin your employment. It's critically important to be on time. A while ago, I was told to report to work between 7:30 a.m. and 8:00 a.m. for my first day. So I figured arriving at 7:45 a.m. would be perfect. To my surprise, although they had given me a range of time to report, I could see they were a bit annoyed by my 7:45 a.m. arrival. I guess I was expected to be at work at 7:30 a.m.! Lesson learned. If you are asked to arrive on your first day at a specific time or within a range of time, I recommend arriving at the earlier time or ten minutes before the specified time.

During your interview and your onboarding process you asked about the company's expectations of you during the first week, first month, and first three months. In some larger companies I have found that it can take quite a while to come up to speed in your new position. In other organizations you may be expected to hit the ground running with little or no learning curve. Perhaps the worst possible situation is not asking questions about expectations and showing up the first day and — surprise — this is not what you had expected. As we discussed in previous chapters, ideally you have asked the right questions about expectations, and you are now on a path to the career that's right for you. Congratulations!

CHAPTER 11

The First Six Months In Your Chosen Position

YOU ARE READY TO BEGIN A NEW POSITION or launch your career. Is this the right choice? Did you make the right decision? Of course, these are questions you will ask yourself. We all second-guess important decisions such as a new position and especially if you decided to transition your career.

Just remember that every decision you make is a right decision! You did your research and made a decision based on your Circle of Acceptance. But that's not the end of the story. Your career is a long-term venture, so it's a good idea to track and analyze each step along the way. During the first six months at your new job you will need to objectively assess whether the path you chose is the right career move for the long term.

As I mentioned in earlier chapters, we often get comfortable in a position and fail to realize this is not the job or career we really want. So make sure that, along with performing at the highest level in your new position, you are also aware that this may or may not be the right choice for you for the long term. Take time to regularly reflect to solidify the choice you made.

But let's not get ahead of ourselves. Tomorrow is your first day on the job! You are excited, nervous, and may even be questioning your decision about your new position. You are experiencing all the normal emotions that we all experience in the days prior to the start date. You want to make a good impression on the first day, so you will need to prepare yourself for all the things you can control. Change is difficult. Even though you made the decision to change positions or take a new job, the change is at best uncomfortable. Yet this is your decision for a new or better career, so take all the good thoughts you can, and make this day the most positive step toward a fulfilling career.

Here are a few tips to ensure your first day of work is comfortable and successful:

- Know how you are going to dress and choose your attire in line with company policy.

- If you are commuting, make sure you know the route and listen to the traffic news in the morning or check out traffic conditions on a traffic app.

- Arrive at your place of work at least ten minutes prior to the time you have been given as a start time.

- During your interview or in the onboarding process you may have been advised what will be expected from you on your first day and during your first week. If you have not been told about these expectations, make sure you speak with your supervisor about his or her expectations of you during this time. In some instances you will:

  - Be introduced to your peers and other management personnel.

  - Be asked to hit the ground running and become a productive part of the company within hours of your reporting time.

- Be instructed to simply become comfortable with your surroundings during your first few days. In larger companies, it can practically take two weeks just to find the bathroom! In the 1990s I went to work for a large company as a senior executive. When I arrived, I was told that there was an emergency and all the senior managers would be out of the office for the next four days. I was shown to a desk with a computer and left on my own. Based on what I knew of my position and the goals I needed to achieve, I simply began working to build my division. By the way, I found the bathroom in about ten minutes.

- In some companies you will be welcomed with openness, while in others you will be met with a standoffish hello from some coworkers and managers. In the latter case, put your best foot forward and try to make everyone comfortable with you and your new position.

- Be aware of your surroundings and understand the work environment. By doing this you will become a comfortable part of the company in a shorter period of time.

In most organizations there is a probationary period of ninety days. The probationary period usually is a non-issue for directors and C-level executives. This is the time a company takes before it begins vesting your benefits and vacation accrual. It is also the time a company will assess your work product. In temp-to-hire positions, this probationary period is the responsibility of a staffing agency.

Also, the first ninety days is the time for *your* assessment. You have worked at the highest level and have dedicated yourself to the quality of your work. At the three-month mark you can assess your desire to continue your employment. If all or most aspects of your position continue to fall within your Circle of Acceptance, then you should continue working another ninety days and, at that time, reevaluate your time at the company. If the situation is acceptable but you are still unsure if this is the right career or company for you, then by all means continue for another ninety days.

If, however, you know this is not the job or career for you — GET OUT! Begin looking for the right job and the right career. If this choice is simply not right for you, don't let your comfort level in this position stop you from taking a step to make a change. Remember, it's your career — it's your choice!

Years ago, I took a job in my chosen career with a company that promised I would be an important part of the organization's management team. I was told I would be president of the division I was helping to create and part of the executive management team of the company. We had extended conversations about my future with the company and the projections for revenue and profit, but I never got it in writing! Too trusting and perhaps too naive. In the first month I was delegated to a minor role in the company, and they promoted someone else as the leader of the division. It took less than ninety days for me to realize there was no future here, and I began looking for other opportunities. I was not going to make another mistake, and it was over a year before I changed positions. I was patient and allowed time to find my next career opportunity.

Keep in mind, though, it is best not to rush to judgement about a company. Even though we have been told that our first impression is usually the right impression, deciding about a company and the people should not be made without your own thoughtful internal analysis. You will know if this chosen company is the right company. Ask yourself, "Is this where I want to be over the next twenty years?" If the answer is no, then it is time to move on.

During the first three months of employment make sure you assess your position, your coworkers, the management style, and the company. Be sure to do this again at the six-month mark. In fact, it's a good idea to do this every thirty days. Remember, this is your career, and by assessing your environment during this initial period, you will ensure you have made the right decision.

As you reflect, ask yourself these questions:

- Does everything you were told about the company, the staff, and the management fall within your Circle of Acceptance?

- If you are making a commute is it acceptable to you?

- Is the job you accepted the right fit for you?

- Are you sure the promises made to you during the interview and the onboarding process are on the right track (for example: work hours, position, management, and knowing your path to promotion)?

- Are you documenting those items that may be different than what you were told or promised?

By regularly assessing your initial term at your new company, you will know within the first few months whether this is the right fit for you. If during this time, you are still questioning your decision, don't make a quick and impetuous decision to leave. If you need to address any issues, request a meeting with management to discuss these issues before they become a problem. Be clear, assertive, objective, and unemotional as you work together to resolve any issues. Most likely, your manager will be motivated to ensure you are happy in your new position, able to be fully productive, and are receiving everything you were promised.

If you feel you have resolved most, if not all, the issues or if you feel these issues can be resolved, make an assessment plan for the next ninety days. Again, it's your career — it's important to continually keep your finger on the pulse.

On the other hand, if the issues cannot be resolved and they fall outside your Circle of Acceptance, it may be time to consider a change. If you are faced with this situation, don't hesitate to start taking steps to move on to a position that is in line with your career goals.

Too many people remain in a position that is "almost right," become comfortable, and BANG! — it's thirty years later and they are with the same company, and they are not happy! I am a prime example of someone who was comfortable, getting promotions, and making good money but was not happy. This is a sacrifice no one should make. Our work — our career — is not a rehearsal. We have only a few chances to choose our careers wisely. Getting stuck in a career that is not the one you want, doesn't make you happy, and will not create the life you dreamed of will only have you looking back years from now saying, "What was I thinking?"

Perhaps you have chosen the right career but have gone to work for the wrong company — the company culture is not what you expected, the management is poor, and the internal politics are untenable. You may determine this in the first three months. Don't just quit — yet don't delay. You need to begin looking for a similar position within the industry with a different company. Delaying your decision to move away from a toxic environment will only make it more difficult the longer you stay.

Alternatively, you may discover in the first three months that the career path you chose is just not right for you. It is now time to consider a new career — one that is more in line with your passions, desires, and goals. Most likely, when you chose your career path, you had two or three options. Revisit your options, conduct additional research, and select a career that is more in line with your goals and passions. I know this decision can be difficult, but eventually you will be in a successful career. You will be able to look back years from now and say, "I made the right decision!"

The first six months in your new position are the most important in planning your future. You will know if this particular position was the right decision. A lot of us get caught up in the newness of our company, and six months can pass by swiftly. Manage your time and objectively look at your position, so you can properly and realistically assess whether this is the right place for you. Now you have a job and a paycheck, so it could become uncomfortable to think about moving to a new position or a new company.

If this position is a fit — that's great! But don't forget to assess your position at regular intervals to stay on top of your career goals and continually move forward on your career path.

If this position is not a fit, don't hesitate, and don't procrastinate — the longer you stay, the harder it will be to make the decision to leave! Of course, don't simply jump at the first opportunity. Every career move should be strategic and thoughtful. Your goal is to find the right company that is both a technical and cultural fit. Not every company will be a perfect match for you. My experience has me looking back over my career and seeing how unhappy I was with my career choice, while at the same time I was afraid to make a significant career move. When I finally made my decision to leave a company (not my career), I made some mistakes along the way, but each time I was able to pick myself up and keep searching for the right company and a position that was a better fit in my career. Don't be afraid to leave a position and make a move to a company that you feel is best for you. In the long run, this will be the correct career move.

Deciding to stay with your new company is a decision that will define an important part of your life. If this is the right choice — stay, prosper, and become a success. If it is not, don't delay — begin to find the career, company, and position that are the best fit for you.

CHAPTER 12
Summary: Bringing It All Together

DOZENS OF WORKSHOPS AND ARTICLES discuss choosing a career, networking, writing a resume, interview techniques, and choosing the right company. This book is written with over seventy years of collective experience in staffing and human resources. Our perspective is unique and informed. The approach we discuss answers your career questions and explains how to navigate the hiring process to achieve your goals. We are confident that by following the principles and guidelines detailed in this book, you will prosper and enjoy your chosen career.

Use this book as your guide to find and build the career that is best for you. Don't settle for anything less than your dream! If you do, you could look back after forty years and say, "What was I thinking? I could have done so much more!"

Making a career choice and navigating the hiring process have dramatically changed in the past thirty years. The hiring process has become impersonal and more difficult as it has evolved from just considering your technical ability and receiving an offer. Companies now consider your cultural and behavioral fit along with your technical skills. Our experience has taught us that a majority of job seekers are not aware of the dynamics and the steps they need to take to be noticed and hired by the company of their choice.

It's Your Career — It's Your Choice gives you a step-by-step approach to decide on a career path and secure the right position with the right company.

You may reach out to a recruiting company (a full-time placement agency or a temporary service organization, also known as *headhunters*) to help you find a position, but always be aware that most of these companies receive a fee for their services, and they are working on behalf of their business clients. Your career is not their first concern. If you feel you need a recruiting company to help you find a position, make sure it is working for you by informing the recruiter or the company that you are seeking a quality career opportunity. But remember, every chapter in this book outlines the simple steps for you to "become your own recruiter"! Besides, no one knows what you want better than you.

Once you have selected your career or decided to transition your career, it is incumbent upon you to understand how to achieve your goal. The preceding chapters outline each step needed for your success. The three most important parts of the process are:

1. Actively networking to make connections.

2. Creating a resume that is concise, readable, and impactful.

3. Using the unique techniques presented in this book to ace your interview.

By following the guidelines in these three areas, you will achieve success in a short period of time. There are also other options available to help you find the industry, company, and position you want. One of those options is Career Coaching.

Career Coaching has been part of the employment scene for decades, but it is still an unregulated industry. Sure, there are numerous organizations that offer Career Coaching certificates but, in reality, someone who wants to be a Coach could, in fact, certify themselves! Coaching certifications range in cost from a few hundred dollars to thousands of dollars. A committed and successful Career Coach will use his or her training as a guide to develop a program that will have a positive result for the clients. Choose a Coach with whom you have a high level of comfort, trust, and synergy. A Career Coach works for you and on your behalf. If you are unemployed and looking for a new position — or seeking a new career — coaching may be the right path for you.

Career Coaching however can be expensive. Coaching programs can range from a few hundred dollars to over ten thousand dollars. Remember, success is not based on the cost of the program — it is based on the quality of the Coach. Paying a huge price for a coaching program will not guarantee success! Also, be aware that some coaching programs commit you for three or six months even if you only need one month of coaching.

Once you select a Career Coach, let the person know what you want from the coaching process (for example: career choice, resume writing, networking assistance, time management, goal setting, or interviewing techniques). This will eliminate any unnecessary time spent on the part of the process you don't need.

For example, if you already know the kind of work you want to do or if you have identified a few companies you want to work for, don't let your coach spend time discussing what you already know! If, however, you don't know the exact career path you want to pursue, make sure your Coach understands that you need assistance in identifying a career.

The career-search and job-search processes discussed in this book can help you make an investment in a Coach who is not beyond your financial means. You may be out of work and need a Coach to assist you in finding a job that you want and is financially rewarding. Select a Career Coach who will work within your budget and is knowledgeable about making a successful career choice and the hiring process. The chapters in this book empower you to research, network, create a resume, and interview with the confidence you need to find the right career and position. If you are considering working with a Career Coach, it is incumbent on you to find a Coach with whom you can connect and who is dedicated to your career.

Career Coaching is an art form. There are hundreds of excellent Coaches who can guide you through the process to find your career. However, some Coaches combine Career Coaching with Life Coaching. Try not to get caught up in an in-depth process that discusses who you think you are and how to improve your life. You can spend unnecessary time that will delay your career search.

Also, be sure the Career Coach you select understands all the elements of selecting a career, identifying the company you want to work for, and most importantly understanding today's hiring process. As mentioned, you need more than an attractive resume to find that right position. Your coaching process should address how to select the right career and how to successfully navigate the hiring process. Perhaps it is time to restate how important it is for you to be honest and forthright when you are discussing your career goals. Most importantly, this is your choice, and your Coach is your guide! Only you can decide the career direction you want to take.

Your decision to start on a path to a new career or transition your career is one of the most important actions you will take in your life. Take time to review the guidance in the previous chapters. Get in touch with your passions and research the companies or industries that interest you. Once you decide on a path, develop a plan of action including a timeframe for success that is aggressive but not impossible to achieve. Use the networking tools in this book to research a company and to gain an understanding of the company and its culture. By using these networking tools, you can almost eliminate the all-too-common situation of landing the "perfect" position only to realize that you are now working in a hostile environment. Your pre-employment networking conversations can help to eliminate any negative surprises you could experience once you begin working at your new company.

If you are transitioning your career, networking is the most important task you will undertake throughout this process. Do you have extensive background in a specific area but are looking to make a significant change? Your resume can outline your experience but does not show the background necessary for the career path you now want to pursue. By networking and speaking to individuals who work in the area you have chosen, you can glean information that will allow you to make an informed decision, and you could possibly find a mentor who will guide you through your transitioning process.

Don't be discouraged if you don't find your chosen company or career quickly. This journey is one of the most important decisions you will make. You may have heard that it takes one month of job or career searching for every $10,000 you earn annually. This may or may not be true for your chosen career, but it is a helpful reminder that the job-search process can take time. Be patient.

Using the processes outlined in this book, we are confident you can substantially decrease the time needed to find the right career, the right company, and the right position. Yes, it may take time, but by following the steps in each chapter you will find the career and position that will define a clear and successful picture of your life.

APPENDIX 1

List Of States That Prohibit Interview Questions On Salary Expectations

As noted in Chapter 7, multiple states, territories, and municipalities have enacted policies or restrictions that prohibit employers from asking interview questions such as, "What are your salary/hourly expectations for this position?"

It's always good to understand what you can and cannot be asked by a potential employer! If you are interviewing in any of these areas and you are asked about your salary expectations or salary history, it is your decision on whether or not to answer the question. As we mentioned in Chapter 7, you could respond by saying, "Before we discuss salary, I would like to know more about the position and the responsibilities, so we can have an open conversation on how I can be an asset to the organization." Or you could say, "I'd like to have an open and honest conversation about salary expectations and your salary range." However, if you state that you know it is illegal to ask about salary, you may run the risk of immediate disqualification from consideration for the position.

Here is a list of states (as well as the District of Columbia and Puerto Rico) that have enacted this prohibition, along with brief details. For an updated list, go to https://www.hrdive.com/news/salary-history-ban-states-list/516662/

- **Alabama** — All employers can't decline hiring, interviewing, promoting, or employing an applicant if they refuse to provide their pay history.

- **California** — All employers can't ask for an applicant's pay history. If they already have the information or the applicant volunteers it, that information can't be used to determine pay. Employers are also required to provide pay scale information if an applicant asks.

- **California** — San Francisco: All (including contractors and subcontractors): Employers can't ask for or use an applicant's compensation when setting pay. Employers also can't disclose a current or former employee's salary without their consent.

- **Colorado** — All employers can't ask for an applicant's pay history. They also can't use pay history to set salaries. They can't discriminate or retaliate against a candidate who doesn't disclose their pay history.

- **Connecticut** — All employers can't ask for an applicant's pay history unless the applicant voluntarily discloses the information.

- **Delaware** — All employers can't screen applicants based on past salary, and they can't ask about salary history. They can verify salary after extending an offer.

- **District of Columbia** — Government agencies can't ask applicants for their salary history unless it's brought up by the candidate after an employment offer is extended.

- **Georgia** — Atlanta City agencies: The city can no longer ask for pay history on its applications, in interviews, or in employment screenings.

- **Hawaii** — All (includes employment agencies) employers can't ask about salary history. They also can't use that information unless the applicant volunteers it. The law doesn't apply to internal applicants.

- **Illinois** — State agencies: The state can't ask applicants about salary history.

- **Illinois** — All employers can't ask about salary history including benefits or other compensation, but they can discuss the applicant's pay expectations.

- **Illinois** — Chicago City departments can't ask for salary history.

- **Kentucky** — Louisville/Jefferson County Metro Government offices and agencies: City offices can't ask for an applicant's salary history.

- **Louisiana** — New Orleans City departments: City offices can't ask for an applicant's salary history. Applicants can provide pay history to negotiate a higher salary after an offer is made.

- **Maine** — All employers can't ask for an applicant's pay history until a job has been offered.

- **Maryland** — All employers can provide an applicant with a wage range for the position and can confirm voluntarily provided salary history once an offer of employment is made. Employers cannot retaliate against an applicant that does not voluntarily provide salary history.

- **Maryland** — Montgomery County: The county can't use salary history to decide whether to hire an applicant. They also can't retaliate against or decline to hire a person who refuses to share their salary history. The county can use salary history to offer a higher salary than initially offered as long as this doesn't result in unequal pay for equal work and the information was voluntarily disclosed.

- **Massachusetts** — All employers can't ask for salary history. They can confirm history if the applicant volunteers or if they've extended an offer.

- **Michigan** — Private employers: Michigan has banned salary history bans.

- **Michigan** — State departments: State offices can't ask an applicant about their salary history until a conditional employment offer is made. They also can't ask current or prior employers or search public records to get that information. If salary is already known, it can't be used to make a hiring decision.

- **Mississippi** — Jackson City offices: City offices can't ask for salary history.

- **Missouri** — All employers can't ask for or use salary history when offering employment or determining salary, benefits, or other compensation. They can discuss the applicant's pay expectations. Prohibitions don't apply to information disclosed by the applicant.

- **Missouri** — Kansas City: City offices can't ask for pay history until the person has been hired.

- **New Jersey** — All employers may not screen applicants based on salary history nor require specific salary history to satisfy a minimum or maximum criteria. Employers may confirm pay history after an offer of employment.

- **New York** — All state agencies and departments (except Port Authority): State offices can't request salary history until after an employment offer is made. If previous compensation is already known, it can't be used to determine an applicant's salary.

- **New York** — Private employers can't ask for salary history. An employer can confirm salary if the applicant gives a pay history to support a higher salary when a job is offered.

- **New York** — New York City: All employers can't ask about previous pay or benefits. If they already have that information, they can't use it to set pay.

- **New York** — Albany County: All employers can't request past compensation information until after a job offer is made.

- **New York** — Suffolk County: All employers can't request past compensation information. They can't search public records or use known salary information to set pay.

- **New York** — Westchester County: All employers can't request past compensation information. They can confirm past pay and use that information in setting pay in certain circumstances.

- **North Carolina** — State agencies can't request salary history and can't use previously obtained salary information to set pay.

- **Ohio** — Cincinnati: State and local governments are excluded, with the exception of Cincinnati employers can't ask for salary history or use known salaries. They're also required to provide a pay scale for a position if the applicant has received an employment offer.

- **Ohio** — Toledo: Employers with fifteen or more employees located in the city: Employers can't ask for pay history. They also can't require an applicant's compensation to satisfy minimum or maximum criteria. They can discuss an applicant's pay expectations.

- **Oregon** — All employers can't ask about pay history until an employment offer has been made. They're also prohibited from using previous salary information to set pay, except for existing employees moving to a new role.

- **Pennsylvania** — State agencies can't ask about current compensation or compensation history. Additionally, all job postings have to clearly disclose a position's pay scale and range.

- **Pennsylvania** — Pittsburgh City offices and agencies: City employers can't ask about prior pay. If they discover the information, they're prohibited from using it unless the applicant has volunteered it.

- **Pennsylvania** — Philadelphia City offices and agencies: City employers cannot inquire about an applicant's wage history or retaliate against an applicant for failing to provide wage history. City employers also cannot rely on wage history in determining wages for an employee unless the applicant willingly disclosed wage history.

- **Puerto Rico** — All employers can't request pay histories, but voluntary salary disclosures made after a job offer has been extended are allowed.

- **South Carolina** — Columbia City agencies: The city can't use pay history unless the applicant voluntarily provides the information.

- **South Carolina** — Richland County has deleted the salary history question from its applications, interviews, and employment screenings.

- **Utah** — Salt Lake City: City offices can't ask applicants about their salary history. If the applicant voluntarily provides the information, it can't be used to determine current salary.

- **Vermont** — All employers can't request pay histories. If the information is volunteered, they can only confirm after making a job offer.

- **Virginia** — All salary history has been removed from state applications.

- **Washington** — State agencies: Employers can't ask for pay history. They can confirm voluntarily disclosed information before or after an offer has been extended.

- **Wisconsin** — All Wisconsin has banned salary history bans.

APPENDIX 2

Worksheet With Additional Interview Questions

In Chapter 7, we noted more than a dozen tough interview questions. Here is an additional list of questions that you could possibly be asked during your interview. We encourage you to review these interview questions, so you can prepare and answer them to the best of your ability. Reviewing the questions and suggested responses in advance enables you to control the part of the interview that is within your control. Remember, always be honest, and don't guess at an answer.

We have presented this section as a worksheet, so you can make notes on your responses and practice before your interview.

Tell me about your successes?

Answer this question with comments about your specific successes and how they relate to the company's needs and values.

_____

_____

_____

Tell me about your education?

Talk only about what you enjoyed and the specific subjects that relate to this position.

_____

_____

_____

Will your qualifications make you a success at our company?

Talk about your skill set and how it relates to the company. Remember to stay on subject and never speak for longer than two or three minutes.

_____

_____

_____

Once hired how long do you think it will be before you can contribute to our company?

Many companies will expect you to make an immediate contribution ("hit the ground running"), so discuss your previous accomplishments and your commitment to getting the job done in a timely manner.

_____

_____

_____

Why should we hire you — why are you the best candidate for the position?

Discuss your research on the company and how your past accomplishments are related to the position. Also discuss that you have selected the company, as you are confident that this is the right career opportunity for you.

_____

_____

_____

Are you considering any other offers?

You should not feel the necessity to reveal any information about other offers or interviews. You can mention that there are other possibilities but, primarily, your interest is in this company.

_____

_____

_____

What would you change in your career?

Make sure you don't become negative. Let them know you are pleased with your past choices. For example, if you want to say that you should have completed college, make sure you conclude by saying you plan to complete your education in the near future (if this is true).

_____

_____

_____

Talk about a situation in which you had a manager with whom you did not agree. How did you handle the situation?

Discuss the communication with the manager and how the situation was resolved. If the situation could not be resolved, try to move the conversation to your accomplishments.

What have you done to increase sales and profit?

This is the perfect time for you to tout your accomplishments as they relate to the new position. Try to cite numbers and percentages.

We are going to conduct references that are both professional and personal. What would your previous managers say about you?

Discuss your previous successes and how your managers were appreciative of your work efforts (work product). You can even discuss that all the projects you were assigned were completed on time (if this is true). Note: Always give a professional reference who will give you a positive review and ask that person for permission to use them as a reference.

_____

_____

_____

What are your future ambitions?

Discuss that this is the company you selected, and you feel you have a future here. Talk about how your work ethic will be an asset to the company and that, over time, you want to grow with the organization. Don't discuss that this position may be a steppingstone for a future position at another company.

_____

_____

_____

Why do you want to work here?

Discuss your research on the company and how you feel the position is perfect for you and that it is a great cultural fit. Your honesty about how the company is right for you will go a long way in the interview.

What kind of hours did you work in your previous positions?

This is simple to answer: "I will do whatever it takes to get the job done." But the answer is not so simple if you only want to work from 8:00 a.m. to 5:00 p.m., forty hours a week. In this case, it is OK for you to ask about overtime or work outside the normal work week. This question could be a deal breaker if you are not willing to work outside the normal work week or if work/life balance is especially important to you.

How much do you think you should earn in this position?

Refer to the Chapter 8's discussion on negotiation and Appendix 1's discussion on answering salary questions.

_____

_____

_____

Were you ever criticized for the work you have accomplished?

Discuss being criticized and immediately segue to what you have learned from the experience. Don't spend too much time on your answer.

_____

_____

_____

Why are you leaving your current position?

Answer this question in as few words as possible. If it was a reduction in force or a layoff, just state that the company experienced a few changes. If you were terminated for cause, try to explain the situation in a positive tone.

_____

_____

_____

How would you rate your previous employer?

Don't be negative! Negativity in an interview can disqualify you from a new position. Discuss the positives of your previous employment (for example, "It was a great company, but it was not a cultural fit for me").

_____

_____

_____

How long will you work for us?

This is a tough question to answer. You can state that you are committed to working for them, and you want to make a meaningful contribution to the company.

_____

_____

_____

How would your coworkers describe you?

Talk about your most positive attributes and how you got along with everyone with whom you worked. Discuss your positive personality traits.

_____

_____

_____

What did you think of your previous manager?

If it was a good relationship tell them how well you got along. If the relationship was less than positive, use uplifting words to describe the situation.

_____

_____

_____

What outside activities do you enjoy?

Be very careful with this one. As we discussed in the chapter on interviewing, discussing your interests and hobbies may not be in line with the interests and hobbies of the interviewers. Try to get an understanding of your audience before you answer. Telling them something that rubs them the wrong way (such as volunteering for a political organization that doesn't align with their views) could be a deal breaker.

_____

_____

_____

When can you start working with us?

If you are interested in the position and an offer has yet to be made, you can ask if they are offering you a position. If there is no formal offer you can give them a tentative start date pending an official offer. If an offer has been made, be prepared to give them the exact date you can start.

Do you have an issue with taking a personality test?

Just let them know that you are comfortable taking a personality test. If you take this test answer the questions as you want to answer them and not what you think the interviewer wants to hear!

Discuss an instance where you worked under pressure and how you handled it?

Discuss your accomplishment in one situation where you effectively met a challenging deadline.

_____

_____

_____

Have you ever been terminated from a company for cause?

If so, this is a tough one! Be careful how you answer the question. Be honest, and try to spin the answer to a positive.

_____

_____

_____

ABOUT THE AUTHORS

MARK BRENNER, SHRM, spent over forty years in the staffing and human resources industry as a recruiter, manager, corporate executive, and business owner. He understands how important it is for every job seeker to make the right career choice, and he has successfully guided thousands of candidates to find the right position with the right company.

After leaving the staffing industry in 2012, Mark became a Career Coach. He has worked with hundreds of clients, helping them to identify the right career and guiding them through each step of the hiring process. Mark has developed unique and successful customized coaching programs that have helped his clients find the career they want. One popular coaching program, an employment-centric improv class, focuses on helping job seekers improve their interviewing skills. Mark is passionate about helping others find the right position by using his unique tools and guidance to navigate the hiring process.

Mark is a U.S. Air Force Vietnam Veteran who created a non-profit organization called Veterans Career Xchange, which coaches Veterans who are transitioning from the military into a civilian career. He has assisted in the transition of over 500 Veterans. His work with Veterans has been recognized by the City of Los Angeles, the State of California, and the United States Congress.

Mark holds a bachelor's degree, a Career Coaching certificate and is an adjunct professor in human resource management at a California state university. As a motivational speaker and trainer, he has presented to groups as large as 500 attendees and has conducted a myriad of workshops on staffing, networking, resume preparation, and interviewing. In addition, he has served on several boards of directors for both nonprofit and for-profit organizations.

MARY GOMEZ is a senior sales executive who has worked with thousands of skilled and non-skilled job seekers, helping them find employment throughout the United States. She has extensive experience working as a liaison between internal and external clientele. She has managed teams of professionals in the staffing, human resources, real estate, and software as a service (SaaS) environments.

Mary has extensive experience coaching, mentoring, and guiding her clients to develop clear, concise, and obtainable career goals. Further, she has mentored, developed, and led multiple sales teams to increase revenue through extensive training programs that she developed. Her experience also includes training, coaching, and mentoring seasoned executive-level professionals. In her recent role as Corporate Director of Client Engagement, Mary talks with thousands of job seekers. She works with professionals who are not sure how to conduct a strategic job search that will yield positive results and guides them to learn and master the steps to success.

Over the course of her professional career, Mary has worked from the ground up to ensure clear understanding between the human resource needs of the company, its hiring goals, the hiring managers' goals and pain points, and the needs of the job seeker. Mary has a hands-on approach and has worked in the trenches; she understands how to fully engage and motivate her clients by educating and guiding candidates to approach their job search differently — not just accepting the status quo. She encourages candidates to use readily available technologies and takes a consultative approach to identify pain points in their current job or career, which ultimately leads to a career choice and not just another job. She has trained candidates on interviewing techniques, how to properly prepare for an interview, and much more.

Mary believes if you have a desire to do something that means you can do it! In addition, she enjoys her role as a board member of the Veterans Career Xchange, working with Veterans to find a fulfilling career after their military service and helping to secure funds for this worthwhile organization.

Milton Keynes UK
Ingram Content Group UK Ltd.
UKHW021312191023
430926UK00026B/1190